The Church of the Living God

THE CHURCH OF THE LIVING GOD

A Reformed Perspective

Wallace M. Alston Jr.

Westminster John Knox Press
LOUISVILLE • LONDON

Unless otherwise indicated, Scripture quotations are from the New Revised Standard Version of the Bible, copyright © 1989 by the Division of Christian Education of the National Council of the Churches of Christ in the U.S.A., and used by permission.

Grateful acknowledgment is made to the following authors and publishers for kind permission to reprint the following previously published material:

Excerpt from *The Piety of John Calvin,* ed. and trans. by Ford Lewis Battles. Copyright 1978 Baker Book House. Used by permission of the Estate of Ford Lewis Battles.

Excerpt from "The Hippopotamus" in *Collected Poems 1909–1962* by T. S. Eliot, copyright 1936 by Harcourt, Inc., copyright 1963, 1964 by T. S. Eliot, reprinted by permission of Faber & Faber Ltd.

Excerpt from "the Cambridge ladies who live in furnished souls." Copyright 1923, 1951, © 1991 by the Truestees for the E. E. Cummings Trust. Copyright © 1976 by George James Firmage, from *Complete Poems: 1904–1962* by E. E. Cummings, edited by George J. Firmage. Used by permission of Liveright Publishing Corporation.

Book design by Sharon Adams
Cover design by Night & Day Design

This book is printed on acid-free paper that meets the American National Standards Institute Z39.48 standard. ♾

PRINTED IN THE UNITED STATES OF AMERICA

02 03 04 05 06 07 08 09 10 11 — 10 9 8 7 6 5 4 3 2 1

Library of Congress Cataloging-in-Publication Data
Alston, Wallace M., 1934–
    The church of the living God : a reformed perspective / Wallace M. Alston, Jr.
      p. cm.
    Includes bibliographical references and indexes.
    ISBN 0-664-22553-5
    1. Church. 2. Reformed Church—Doctrines. I. Title.

BV600.3 .A47 2002
262'.042—dc21   2001043784

For Alice

Contents

Chapter 1

The Church for Such a Time

The church of Jesus Christ is a strange affair, a mixed bag we might say today, a mixed body *(corpus mixtum)* as Augustine put it in the second decade of the fifth century. On the one hand, the church is an organization, an institution, a form of human association like any other. On the other hand, if we are to believe the things often said about it, the church is completely different, without analogy or parallel, absolutely unique. What to do with this paradox?

On the surface of things, the church does not appear to be so complex and complicated. Judging from outward appearances, in fact, the church is as familiar and explicable to us as any other organization or institution in society, be it a school, a corporation, or a political party. The church can actually be located on a map; it usually occupies an identifiable building; it transacts its business by means of the common currency; it organizes itself and functions alongside other forms of human association with little to distinguish it from them.

Many people who belong to the church, however, believe that there is more to the church than the unaided eye can see. They are convinced that the church cannot be adequately identified or explained in empirical terms alone. They claim that the mystery of the church, which accounts for its apparently paradoxical existence, is seen only through the eyes of faith. They acknowledge that the church is a human institution, but they go on to affirm that the church is the creation and gift of God. The story of the church, they would have us believe, is the story of God's creating and restorative activity in the world, from Adam and Eve to Jesus Christ, and from him to the likes of you and me.

The apostle Paul sets this paradox in context in 1 Timothy 3:15 where he refers to the church as "the church of the living God, the pillar and bulwark of the truth." He takes a verbal sight on the two sides of the church's existence and in so doing leaves us a context for our discussion of that particular part of the church commonly known as Reformed. From one point of view, the church is a pillar, planted deep in the soil of the past, which is capable of supporting the weight of a significant foundation. The church is also a bulwark, in or behind which one may find refuge from threat or harm. But, according to Paul, that is only part of the story. The rest of the story is that of the church of the living God, who comes to us from out of the future, picks up the pieces of the past, and leads us by way of one exodus or another, one resurrection or another, in the traverse of a present full of promise. This is the context in which the paradox of the church finds its fit. Thus, it makes sense to pause here before we move on to identify the ecclesiology of a particular historical tradition.

THE PILLAR AND BULWARK OF THE TRUTH

The church is a pillar and bulwark of the truth. Does this mean that the church has a monopoly on the truth, that its doctrines and creeds contain the truth, the whole truth, and nothing but the truth? Is there no truth worth believing anywhere else, as in other philosophies or religions? Must people who belong to the church believe what the church tells them to believe about God, Jesus, the Bible, ethical and moral issues, and so on? Are we not to run these things through our own minds and hearts, testing them against the other things we know and believe, until their truth is either confirmed or rejected?

Martin Luther is said to have told the story of a peasant who was asked by a stranger what he believed. "What the church believes," the peasant replied. Luther commented that the man could not possibly have been saved. No one, least of all the church, can do another's believing just as no one can do another's dying. In one sense, which we shall later mention, the church does do our believing for us, but in the end each of us must give our own account of the hope that is in us. Each of us must finally work out our own salvation with fear and trembling, conscious that God is at work in us both to will and to work for God's good pleasure (Phil. 2:12–13).

And yet, it is encouraging to know that we do not have to do that *de novo* in every new generation. We have the witness of the church, a great and long history of believing, the testimony of men and women in times past who tested the faith and found it to be sound, to guide, strengthen, correct, and fortify us against the various distortions that our own nature so willingly designs. We not only have the faith of the church beneath us as a pillar on which to construct our life's foundation; we have it as a bulwark, a place of refuge and succor when we grow faint of heart or slack of soul.

In fact, the church today has far more cause than Paul had to rejoice in the church as the pillar and bulwark of the truth. We have now, not forty or fifty, but nearly two thousand years of it behind and beneath us—generation after generation of men and women who have believed and lived the gospel in their own time and handed it down to us.

It will be incumbent on the church in an increasingly secular, pluralistic, multicultural world to recall and to reclaim its history of believing if the church is to be clear in its own mind about what the truth really is. The truth that Paul likens to a pillar and a bulwark may be called to mind by a rehearsal of some of the texts that have borne it from one generation to the next, texts such as:

In the beginning when God created the heavens and the earth . . .
(Gen. 1:1)

In the beginning was the Word, and the Word was with God, and the Word was God. . . . And the Word became flesh and lived among us . . . full of grace and truth.
(John 1:1, 14)

The LORD is my shepherd, I shall not want. . . . Even though I walk through the darkest valley, I fear no evil; for you are with me.
(Ps. 23:1, 4)

For God so loved the world that he gave his only Son, so that everyone who believes in him may not perish but may have eternal life.
(John 3:16)

For I handed on to you as of first importance what I in turn had received: that Christ died for our sins in accordance with the scriptures, and that he was buried, and that he was raised on the third day in accordance with the scriptures, and that he appeared to Cephas, then to the twelve.
(1 Cor. 15:3–5)

Therefore, since we are justified by faith, we have peace with God through our Lord Jesus Christ.
(Rom. 5:1)

Son, your sins are forgiven.
(Mark 2:5)

He has told you, O mortal, what is good; and what does the LORD require of you but to do justice, and to love kindness, and to walk humbly with your God?
(Mic. 6:8)

Do not let not your hearts be troubled. . . . In my Father's house there are many dwelling places. . . . I go to prepare a place for you.
(John 14:1–2)

And the peace of God, which surpasses all understanding, will guard your hearts and your minds in Christ Jesus.
(Phil. 4:7)

Thumbing through my grandmother's Bible one day, I found those words underlined ("And the peace of God, which passeth all understanding," KJV) and dated (Feb. 12, 1936), with a note written in the margin after her husband, my grandfather, died. The note said: "This peace passing all understanding came to me the next morning after David died and I felt I could stand it. It never left me. This is June 12, 1944."

These texts are arbitrarily chosen; there are others that might have been cited. They are a fair summary, however, of the truth upon which the existence of the church rests, the word that the church has to speak which will not be spoken if the church does not speak it, the message of hope which people still need to hear despite the attractions and detractions of the contemporary world. It is the truth that has found its proper response in hymns such as "I Greet Thee Who My Sure Redeemer Art," "A Mighty Fortress Is Our God," "How Firm a Foundation," "Now Thank We All Our God," "O God, Our Help in Ages Past," "Be Thou My Vision," and many others. Texts and hymns such as these, along with the great creeds, prayers, and the several liturgies of the church, speak of and have become the pillar and bulwark of the truth, which has enabled ordinary people over the centuries to live with grace, serenity, and a fair measure of grit amid the manifold vissitudes of life.

This faith is our heritage as members of the church, bequeathed to us by the grace of God, to be sure, but also by this ambiguous, compromised, paradoxical occasion we call the church. We are its trustees with a fiduciary responsibility to the future, called and commissioned, if for nothing else, for the task of passing it on with a good measure of love and care to generations yet to come.

THE CHURCH OF THE LIVING GOD

The church is not only the pillar and bulwark of the truth. It is also, and more importantly, the church of the living God, who led the people of Israel out of the land of bondage with a pillar of cloud by day and fire by night, who raised Jesus from the dead, and who, far from being merely a fact of the past, is the determining factor in personal and public life today. The church of the living God is a human community that lives at the beck and call of a will and purpose beyond its ken, a people responding to a living presence who is the one with whom all people daily have to do, who is always moving ahead into a future of challenge and adventure. This was the experience of the early church. Surely the recovery of that experience is important for the church today.

It has been said that the church today faces a first-century situation. It is increasingly a minority community; it lives in a secular, pluralistic world; it no longer occupies a privileged position in the academy. What's more, it is widely reported that something has happened, or is happening, to the intellectual and cultural world in which the contemporary church is called to live. It is said that we are moving out of the modern into a postmodern era, in which many of the assumptions on which the modern world was based are being challenged or altogether denied.

Just what postmodernism is, whether it is real or imaginary, and if real, just what sort of challenge and adventure it has in store for the church, is difficult to say. The word means different things to different people. The most common meaning of *postmodern* is supplied by the so-called deconstructionists, and specifically by the philosopher Jacques Derrida, with whose name the word is regularly associated. For Derrida and the deconstructionists, who denounce all absolutes in favor of a pluralism of meanings and interpretations, everything is a text. Because any given word can have many different meanings depending on the context in which it is used, any text can be read in many different ways. When we read a text, what we find is different meanings playing off against each other.

Two editorials in the *New York Times* illustrate postmodernist thinking and the degree to which it has scaled the wall of academia and made its home in the general discourse of the culture. One editorial, titled "Science Set Free from Truth," likens postmodernism to a mutant virus that has infected not only philosophy and the social sciences but even such alleged bastions of truth and objectivity as physics and chemistry. The author, John Horgan, a senior writer at *Scientific American,* quotes a Belgian chemist who declared that we have reached "the end of certitude." He also notes the claim of a famous physicist to the effect that reality is really a participatory phenomenon, defined by the questions we put to it. He cites the assertion of philosopher Thomas Kuhn that science reflects not the truth about nature but merely scientists' prevailing mindset, which is always subject to change. Horgan argues that this point of view cannot withstand scrutiny, but he does not deny that it has gained considerable currency in our time.[1]

The other editorial, titled "History as Therapy: A Dangerous Idea," finds Arthur Schlesinger Jr. arguing against the incursion of postmodernism into the realm of history. He quotes John Lothrop Motley, the nineteenth-century Dutch historian, who, at a meeting of the New York Historical Society in 1868, said: "There is no such thing as human history. Nothing can be more profoundly, sadly true. The annals of mankind have never been written. . . . We have a leaf or two torn from the great book of human fate as it flutters in the storm-winds ever sweeping across the earth. We decipher them as best we can with purblind eyes, and endeavor to learn their mystery as we float along to the abyss; but it is all confused babble, hieroglyphics of which the key is lost." Schlesinger comments that these postmodernist sentiments express what many contemporary historians fear in the dark night of the soul, namely, that history is, in an ultimate sense, impossible; that the past is past, beyond recovery; and that objectivity is an illusion. While Schlesinger argues vehemently for the distinction between history and fiction, the urgency of his rhetoric betrays his concern that postmodernist thinking is increasingly pervasive in the world today.[2]

Diogenes Allen, in his discussion of "the end of the modern world," views the postmodern phenomenon as an opportunity for Christian witness and wonders if the church is up to the task.[3] Allen characterizes the postmodern as the crumbling of the pillars of a secular universe erected during the Enlightenment. The most fundamental pillar to fall is the commonly accepted philosophical and scientific claim that we live in a self-contained, self-explanatory universe. The second is the assumption that a basis for personal and social morality can be constructed without reference to transcendence. The third is the belief in inevitable progress. The fourth is the assumption that knowledge is inherently good. To these four, I would add others: the assumption that power and authority are most effectively employed when centralized and exercised from the top; the assumption that the future of the family is a future of options, that the disappearance of the marriage culture poses no threat to the health of the social order or to the nourishing and flourishing of children; and the assumption that life is to be ordered according to the prerogatives of the autonomous individual.

This, or something like this, is the world into which the church is being drawn out. Annie Dillard writes,

> On the whole, I do not find Christians, outside the catacombs, sufficiently sensible of the conditions. Does anyone have the foggiest idea what sort of power we so blithely invoke? Or, as I suspect, does no one believe a word of it? The churches are children playing on the floor with their chemistry sets, mixing up a batch of TNT to kill a Sunday morning. It is madness to wear ladies' straw hats and velvet hats to church; we should be wearing crash helmets. Ushers should issue life preservers and signal flares; they should lash us to our pews. For the sleeping god may wake some day and take offense, or the waking god may draw us out to where we can never return.[4]

The question is whether the church will rise to the challenge, whether the church will withdraw or embrace the world into which it is being drawn out as its own peculiar adventure. Within the tradition of which the church is the trustee, there is a wealth of resources upon which to draw, not the least of which is the conviction that the God of whom the tradition speaks is a living God who is alive and active in purposeful ways in the affairs of the postmodern world.

Three strategies commend themselves to the church for such a time. One is an attitudinal strategy, namely, that of quiet confidence about the future. In contrast to the cynicism of those who have grown discouraged and given up on the church, people who trust the living God are confident that its times of faithfulness and effectiveness are not all in the past but lie yet ahead. The dissolution of the hegemony of science, which once made belief in God something of an intellectual embarrassment, particularly in the academy but also in popular culture, has opened the door to conversation between scientists, philosophers, and theologians on such issues as the ultimate reference of empirical data. "The more I examine the universe and the details of its architecture," says Freeman Dyson, "the more evidence I find that the universe in some sense must have known we were coming." In response to which John Polkinghorne comments, "I cannot see what sense that could be other than the will of a Creator."[5] The discoveries and reflections of scientists are leading them to ask questions that science itself cannot answer, such as the ancient query of why there is something and not nothing. And theologians are being accorded opportunities to learn from scientists details of the natural world that suggest a certain correspondence with the articles of faith.

Likewise, the failure of the Enlightenment experiment to construct a moral order, both personal and public, by reason alone without reference to God leaves the cultural door ajar for renewed conversation concerning moral claims that have their origin in will and design beyond the realm of reason. The breakdown of belief in inevitable progress, occasioned by our inability to eradicate such threats to world community as racism, sexism, homophobia, poverty, crime, terrorism, and war, begs for the contemporary recovery of those insights into the nature of the human creature and the future of the human prospect carried by the Judeo-Christian tradition. When all is said and done, our attitude concerning the future of the church will depend on whether we believe in the living God, or whether we are like those "Cambridge ladies who live in furnished souls," of whom e e cummings said, "they believe in Christ and Longfellow, both dead."[6]

A second strategy that has promise for the church for such a time is prayerful expectancy that the living God, by the power of the Spirit at work within, will again renew and reform the church. Prayer, whether we pray and what we pray for, testifies to what we really believe about God. Professor Thomas F. Torrance once said to me that he seldom approved a person for the doctor's degree at the University of Edinburgh until he had heard the person pray. When you listen to a person pray, he said, you discover how good a theologian the person really is, what the person really knows, and what the person really believes. The church of the living God cannot be planned or programmed. We do plan and program, of course, but we do so knowing all the while that what is planned and programmed, if it is in accord with God's will, will be given not forced. The renewal of the church is never a human work but always a gift for which we must wait and pray.

Finally, the church can do no better than to be diligent in the pursuit of those ways and means of building and upbuilding the church that have warrant in the Bible and that have been used by God in times past to equip the church for service—worship, preaching, the administration of the sacraments, Bible study, teaching, the cure of souls, the encouragement of love for one another, stewardship, prophetic critique of social ills and public evils, and a ministry to people in need. These are the means by which the living God has given new life to the church in days gone by and there is no reason to believe that they will not be the means by which God does so again.

There are many ways of being "the church of the living God, the pillar and bulwark of the truth," and people regularly identify themselves with reference to the various historical families that represent these several ways. Thus, it is to the identity of the Reformed Christian to which we now turn.

Chapter 2

The Identity
of the Reformed Christian

*The catholic or universal Church, which is invisible, consists of the
whole number of the elect, that have been, are, or shall be gathered
into one, under Christ the head thereof; and is the spouse, the body,
the fullness of Him that filleth all in all.*

*The visible Church, which is also catholic or universal under
the gospel (not confined to one nation, as before under the law),
consists of all those throughout the world that profess the true religion, together with their children, and is the Kingdom of the Lord
Jesus Christ, the house and family of God, through which men are
ordinarily saved and union with which is essential to their best
growth and service.*

Westminster Confession of Faith

People regularly identify themselves. They identify themselves in order to understand themselves, to communicate with other people, and to establish significant
relationships. They identify themselves by family, by profession or place of
employment, by age, by religious affiliation, and by many other things. Christian people identify themselves for the same reasons: to understand themselves,
to communicate with other people, and to establish significant relationships with
other Christians. What is the Reformed tradition? How do people who belong
to the Reformed tradition identify themselves?

Most of us live in cities or towns in which there are many churches of different denominations. Once it was relatively easy to tell people apart. Denominational traditions were preserved in churches of the various historical traditions, and
members of these churches could be expected to reflect their religious traditions

in their daily lives. Protestants, for example, knew what distinguished them from Roman Catholics. Roman Catholics believed in the authority of the pope, went to confession, attended mass, and ate fish on Friday. Other denominational distinctions were equally clear. Quakers and Christian Scientists had no ministers; Baptists held revivals and Methodists signed temperance pledges. Presbyterians simply looked like Presbyterians. They were clean and well starched. They went to Sunday school and believed in predestination. These distinctions, somewhat caricatured here, nevertheless were very important and widely known.

This is much less so today. Protestant attitudes toward Roman Catholics have changed from condemnation to acceptance and profound respect. Roman Catholicism itself has undergone considerable change since the Second Vatican Council, enabling Roman Catholics to live more comfortably and cooperatively with Protestants. Protestants and Roman Catholics today find themselves in agreement on many things that once divided them, and efforts are being made to achieve intercommunion and mutual recognition of ordination.

The same process of obscuring and relativizing the historical differences of emphasis and experience has taken place within Protestantism itself, particularly in America. This has resulted in an American religion-in-general in which churches of all denominations and historical traditions participate. Distinctions and differences have been so played down, in fact, that sometimes it is hard to know whether one is sitting in a Baptist, Methodist, or Presbyterian church on a given Sunday morning. The orders of worship, hymns, prayers, and language of faith are similar, if not identical. They acknowledge common histories and historical figures, pay lip service to the doctrinal insights of many of the same theologians, and work together in local councils of churches. They all affirm faith in one God, the centrality of Jesus Christ, the presence of the Holy Spirit, the authority of the Bible, the importance of the church, and the ethical urgency of Christian living. Their organizational life and institutional forms, their architecture and vestments, may vary. Some have bishops, others do not. Some have strong regional and national ties to denominations, others do not. To the average layperson, if there be such, these differences now appear to be relatively minor, not divisive or disruptive to the essential unity and identity of the church. People moving into a new community will "shop around" for a church, much as they shop for other things. They will join the church, regardless of denomination, that best meets their needs or those of their family. If the ecumenical movement sometimes appears to be dormant in denominational boards and agencies, it is nonetheless very much alive in the everyday experience of the laity. Protestant churches of all denominations are filled with men and women who have transferred from churches of other denominations, for whom denominational distinctions are lost or unknown.

This grassroots ecumenism is healthy in many ways and may yet lead the several churches into a more inclusive experience of the Christian community at the denominational level. However, it has tended to obscure the historic distinctions of the various Christian families of faith. It is healthy, for example, for my family to sense its commonality with other families in our community. It would make no sense for me to tell my children over and over again how different we are from other families. That would tend to divide us from other families, precluding our sharing the many joys of the common life. On the other hand, being a member of our family is not identical to being a member of some other family. Our family has a different history. We share different experiences. We even eat different food. Similarly, it makes no sense to celebrate denominational differences. Christian unity has long been hampered by denominational pride. Yet being a member of the Reformed family is not identical to being a member of the Episcopal or Baptist family. We have a different history. We share different experiences. We may not eat different food, but we are nourished by different aspects of the Christian faith. What is distinctive about the church in the Reformed family? How do we identify ourselves in that tradition today?

First, we need to be clear about our priorities. To be a member of a church in the Reformed tradition is not, first of all, to be a disciple of John Calvin or an advocate for the Presbyterian form of government. The prior commitment is the commitment to Jesus Christ. The first thing that must be said about who we are as participants in the Reformed tradition is that we are Christians: believers in Jesus Christ and members of the church, the people of God. "Of course, I stand in the Reformed tradition," declared Karl Barth, the great theologian of the twentieth century, "but I believe, as Calvin did, that there is only one Master in the church and in the world. Consequently, I try to be obedient to Christ and not to Calvin."[1] To identify ourselves, first of all, as Christians is to identify ourselves from the beginning with Christ. It is to join the ranks of men and women in every time and place who confess that Jesus is Lord and Savior. It is to assert that all other distinctions and differences, though important, are secondary, that the One who unites us is more significant by far than anything that divides us.

Second, once that has been said, we can go a step further in our attempt to identify ourselves as Reformed Christians, for we are not only Christians in general, but Christians who share a particular history. Of course, we share 1500 years of that history with the Roman Catholic Church. Their heroes and martyrs, theologians and saints, during those 1500 years belong to us and to our history as well. But on October 31, 1517, Martin Luther, a German monk, nailed ninety-five theses to the door of the castle church at Wittenberg and another chapter of Christian history began. The Protestant movement, of which the Reformed churches are a part, began. Thus, although we are Christians in general, we can be more specific and say that we are Protestant Christians in particular.

We cannot tell the story of the Protestant Reformation here. It is important, however, to mention enough of that story to enable us to understand what the word *Protestant* means. We look back on October 31, 1517, as a very dramatic moment in the history of the church, but if someone had recorded the event on film, chances are that it would not be seen as dramatic at all. The Ninety-five Theses, which Luther nailed to the door of the castle church on that day, amounted to ninety-five short propositions concerning the medieval church that

Luther wanted to debate. No one took the occasion seriously enough to attend. This is not to say that the Ninety-five Theses were unimportant. To the contrary, they contained matters of life and death, such as the nature of salvation, the centrality of grace, and the unethical practices of the medieval church. It is to say that Luther did not intend to destroy the church but to debate and to reform the church. Luther had no idea of starting a new religion or of founding a new church. He wanted to retrieve the old religion and revive the old church. His desire was not to break with the past but to reestablish continuity with the apostolic faith recorded in the New Testament and confessed in the ancient creeds.

The Lutherans were first called "Protestants" at the Diet of Speyer in 1529. That assembly outlawed Luther and his followers, and in response they drew up a Protestation, which affirmed the centrality of God's grace and the authority of the Bible. The word *Protestant,* therefore, is not a negative word. It has negative connotations in that one who is for something is by definition against its opposite. But the Latin *protestant* actually means to testify on behalf of something, to engage in a positive witness to something. The first Protestants were people who stood against the abuses of the medieval church because they affirmed the apostolic faith contained in Scripture and confessed in the early Christian creeds. When we identify ourselves as Protestants, therefore, we identify ourselves with a particular understanding of the church. In the minds of some, the church was not reformable. Reforms might happen in the church, but the church itself had no need of major surgery. Those who were labeled "Protestants," however, felt that the church must always be reformed by the Word of God. Repentance and renewal are always necessary for the church and its institutional forms, as well as for individual Christians. They believed that the church continually lives under God's judgment, that judgment begins with the household of God, and that God is constantly reforming and renewing the church. To be a Protestant is to share this doctrine of the church. And, from a human point of view, it is to accept one's own responsibility for the reformation of the church, which began but did not end on October 31, 1517.

Third, we are Protestant Christians of the Reformed tradition. Within Protestantism there are many traditions or families, each with its own particular history and historical personalities. In a very general sense, of course, all Protestants are reformed people, for they trace their origin back to those who sought the reform of the medieval church. Soon after 1517, however, the word *Reformed* began to be used in a more specific sense to refer to the particular reform movement that occurred in Switzerland. Reformed Protestants are people who trace their origins back to the Swiss Reformation.

The Swiss Reformers—Huldrich Zwingli (Zurich), John Calvin (Geneva), Heinrich Bullinger (Zurich), John Oecolampadius (Basel), Berthold Haller (Bern), and others—were more radical in their reforming work than were the Lutherans in Germany. Luther sought to eliminate those beliefs and practices in the medieval church that the Bible specifically condemned. The Swiss Reformers wanted a more thorough reformation of the church. They sought to eliminate those beliefs and practices that the Bible did not specifically require. This may seem to be a distinction without a difference, but not so. The Lutheran Reformation was a more conservative movement in that it allowed more of the medieval church to remain intact. The motto might have been: If the Bible does not prohibit it, keep it. The Swiss Reformation was more open to change in organizational and institutional forms, liturgy and doctrine, and the relationship between church and state. Its motto might have been: If the Bible does not require it, get rid of it. Thus, the word *Reformed* came to refer to the more radical reform movement of Switzerland, which soon spread to Holland, Scotland, England, France, Hungary, Germany, and America.

The word *Presbyterian* narrows the focus of one's Christian identity even more. This word refers to a specific form of government under which many Reformed communities have organized their church life. Reformed people have lived happily under several forms of church government: congregational, episcopal, and presbyterian. New England Congregationalists are Reformed people living under a congregational polity. The Reformed Church of Hungary is a Reformed community living under an episcopal system. The word *presbyterian* has to do with the form of government that has been especially appealing to Reformed people. It is a government by presbyters or elders, elected by the people and serving in governing bodies.

In the seventeenth century, church government became the subject of considerable controversy in Great Britain. The Church of England organized itself under an episcopal polity, while the Church of Scotland elected the presbyterian or representative form of government. Members of the Church of Scotland soon began to refer to themselves as Presbyterians. Likewise, when they came to America, they called their churches Presbyterian. Presbyterians represent one tradition or family within the Protestant movement. To be a Presbyterian is to be a Protestant Christian of the Reformed tradition who lives with others of the same persuasion in a church that is organized under a representative form of government.

Finally, in order to identify ourselves as Christians, we go on to say that we belong to a certain denomination and to a particular congregation of that denomination. Being a Christian in the Reformed tradition is a particular as well as a general commitment. It is a commitment to the life and work of a particular denomination and congregation as well as to a tradition with roots in the past. Although many Protestant denominations (Congregationalist, Baptist, and Episcopal, among others) have been influenced by the Reformed tradition, most Reformed Christians align themselves with denominations that include some specific reference to that tradition in their name. In many parts of the world, denominations that trace their history to the Swiss Reformation still use the name Reformed (e.g., the Reformed Church of France, the Dutch Reformed Church, the United Reformed Church in England). It is important to remember that wherever *Reformed* appears in a church's name, that church in some way traces its history back to the Swiss Reformation. The vast majority of Reformed Christians in the United States, however, and those in other countries to which American and Scottish missionaries have gone, identify with some Presbyterian denomination.

The fact that the church of Jesus Christ is divided into many denominations is an ambiguous fact at best. Jesus prayed that the church might be one, "so that the world may believe" that God had sent him into the world (John 17:21). Some people feel that denominations are a scandal, that they obscure the unity of the church for which Jesus prayed, and that they should be abolished. At times, denominations have obscured the unity of the church and they often do today. When one denomination claims to be spiritually superior to another, when one denomination will not recognize the ordination of another, or when denominations refuse to join together in worship and work, the unity of the church is obscured. But denominations may also play a useful and positive role in maintaining the unity of the church. The church is not uniform but diverse, and we must assume that diversity is a gift of God. There are varieties of Christians with a variety of needs, and there are many valid interpretations and styles of Christian faith and life. There are many legitimate ways to worship God, many valid styles of personal devotion, and many avenues of Christian service, more than any one denomination could ever happily incorporate. Denominations openly acknowledge, accommodate, and honor this great variety in the Christian church. If they were abolished, or if uniformity were coerced, it is likely that other groupings would arise to take their place. Perhaps denominationalism itself is neither good nor bad but rather a fact of life in the contemporary church. The test of all denominational practice is whether it honors diversity and practices inclusiveness without obscuring the essential unity of the church.

The conclusion of our discussion of the identity of the Reformed Christian brings us back full circle to our primary identity as believers in Jesus Christ. We have seen that Reformed Christians identify themselves first as Christians, then as Protestant Christians, then as Reformed Protestants, and finally as members of particular denominations and congregations. To be a Reformed Christian is to confess primary loyalty to Christ and unity with all others who do the same. To identify ourselves, therefore, is to affirm the priority of our ecumenical commitment to all purely sectarian loyalties. Reformed churches, since the very beginning of the movement, have sought the wider Christian union as a witness to the lordship of Jesus Christ. John T. McNeill, a Reformed church historian, wrote that "all the greater Reformers, with the exception of Luther in certain moods and special crises, were consistent advocates either of a Protestant or of a wider Christian union."[2] Sometimes Reformed Christians have forgotten that, although the Protestant Reformation brought disunity to the church, there is a unitive, conciliar, ecumenical commitment at the heart of their tradition, reflecting the conviction that Jesus Christ is Lord.

> The Reformed churches from the beginning defined the church primarily in terms of the action of God in word and sacrament, not in terms of structures or even correct doctrine. This doctrine of the church enabled Reformed communities to recognize the ministries, sacraments, and memberships of other churches. No major Christian community has been more ecumenical in this sense, or more

open in recognition of other Christian ministries, sacraments, and memberships.[3]

Reformed churches throughout the world have found a sense of unity in the World Alliance of Reformed Churches. Reformed and Presbyterian churches in the United States have been active in the formation of ecumenical councils and consortia at regional, national, and international levels. Most Reformed Christians in America can identify themselves not only by denomination but with Christians in this country and across the world through agencies such as the Consultation on Church Union, the National Council of the Churches of Christ in the United States of America, and the World Council of Churches. Reformed churches are always striving for new ways to manifest the centrality of Jesus Christ and the unity of his church throughout the world.

Chapter 3

The Story of the Church

We most surely believe that God preserved, instructed, multiplied, honored, adorned, and called from death to life his Kirk in all ages since Adam until the coming of Christ Jesus in the flesh.

Scots Confession

In his familiar hymn, "God of Grace and God of Glory," Harry Emerson Fosdick wrote:

> God of grace and God of glory,
> On Thy people pour Thy power;
> Crown Thine ancient Church's story;
> Bring her bud to glorious flower.

What is the ancient church's story? Is the story of the church simply the mechanical retelling of the historical events of its past? History is important for anyone who wants to understand the church. It is necessary to know certain historical facts if one is to understand the process by which the church came to be, what it has done through the years, and how it has reflected on its own nature and mission. But historical facts alone do not add up to the ancient church's story. Facts need interpretation if they are adequately to reflect the historical experience of a people.

There are two ways, for example, that one might speak of a person who has been blind and later came to see. A scientific history can describe what happened to the optic nerve or to the crystalline lens, what technique the surgeon used to correct the problem, what medicines were used in the process of the cure, and what stages of recovery the patient passed through. This is important information for anyone who wants to know the blind person. But if the blind person wrote the story herself, the autobiography might be very different. It might make only passing reference to scientific facts and procedures, dwelling instead on her experience of those facts and their meaning for her life. She might write of what it felt like to live in total darkness, and of the newfound joy of seeing the trees and the sunrise, children's faces, and the smiles of friends. The scientific account is the outer history of what happened, while the autobiography is the inner history, which tells of the meaning of what happened.[1] One is an objective rehearsal of the facts; the other is the interpretive story of an individual's life. Both are important for anyone who wants to know the person. The story of the church is a story that includes both the objective facts and the autobiographical interpretation of what these facts mean to people who believe.

How then do we tell the story of the church? Where does the story begin? It is important to know where the story begins, because the beginning affects the way we understand everything else that follows. If we believe that the church began at the initiative of a few lonely men and women in the first century who sought a fellowship of like minds for the facing of a difficult and dangerous time, we will tend to interpret the past, present, and future of the church in one way. But if we believe that the church originated in God's initiative—if God had the church in mind from the beginning, called it into being, sustained it, and willed it to be the instrument of the divine purpose for the world—then we will tend to interpret the past, present, and future of the church in quite another way indeed.

Since Reformed Christians have always placed great emphasis on the authority of the Bible as the Word of God, we might expect them to turn to the Bible for their answer to the question of where the story begins. But turning to the Bible is itself no simple affair. It is increasingly popular these days in Reformed liturgical practice for the minister, following the reading of Scripture, to say, "The Word of the Lord," sometimes even elevating the Bible in full view of the worshiping congregation, which responds, "Thanks be to God." This practice is not without danger of misinterpretation by a congregation that does not understand the nuanced way in which the Bible is identified as the Word of God. We must be clear about what we mean when we say that the Bible is the Word of God, since what we mean by that equation will determine how we identify and define the church. If we mean, or give the impression in liturgical practice that we mean, that the words of the Bible are the very words of God, our doctrine of the church will likely be quite limited if not very narrow. Women will have to be restricted in their participation. They will have to remain silent. They will not be allowed to teach in the church school. They certainly will not be permitted to serve on a church board or to be ordained for ministry (1 Tim. 2:12). They may not even become deacons in the church, for the Bible says that a deacon must be the husband of one wife (1 Tim. 3:12). To take another example, it is not explicitly stated in the New Testament that children are to be baptized or admitted to the sacrament of the Lord's Supper. When we encourage the full participation of women in the church, baptize children, and admit them to the Lord's Table, the tacit assumption is that the words of the Bible are not literally and infallibly the words of God.

The Word of God is not a book. It is God's creative and redeeming activity that makes things happen in the world, calling into being that which is not and making old things new. The world was created by the Word of God, according to Genesis 1. God said, "Let there be . . . ," and there was. The Gospel of John asserts that God's creative and redeeming Word became flesh in Jesus Christ and dwelt among us in a human being. Jesus Christ is the incarnate Word of God, God's creative and redeeming activity that makes things happen. When Reformed Christians speak of the Bible as the Word of God, they mean (or ought to mean) that it is through the Bible that God's creative and redeeming Word, Jesus Christ, comes home to us and lives in our experience. In this derivative sense, the Bible is the written Word, the sacraments of Baptism and the Lord's Supper are the enacted Word, and the sermon and its preaching are the proclaimed Word. But all of these are subordinate to the Word of God, Jesus Christ. Therefore, when we go to the Bible for the answer to the question of where the story of the church begins, we must read those ancient words in the light of Jesus Christ, interpreting the facts of the past, the conditions of the present, and the expectations for the future in the light of what we know and believe about him.

WHERE THE STORY BEGINS

The Bible does not explicitly tell us where the story of the church begins. It leaves the question open to several possible answers. It might be argued, for example, that the church began when Jesus called the Twelve and sent them into the world as his representatives. It might be said that the church began at the foot of the cross, when Jesus entrusted his friends and family to each other and made of them an extended family of faith: "When Jesus saw his mother and the disciple whom he loved standing beside her, he said to his mother, 'Woman, here is your son.' Then he said to the disciple, 'Here is your mother.' And from that hour the disciple took her into his own home" (John 19:26–27). Or it might be argued that the church began when God raised Jesus from the dead. Without the resurrection, the crucifixion of Jesus would have so disappointed the hopes of the disciples as to have returned them to their previous faith convictions and expectations. Yet again, many people have referred to Pentecost as the birthday of the church, for on this occasion the people were collected and empowered for mission by the Holy Spirit. At first glance, the New Testament appears to give us no more than an ambiguous answer to the question of where the story of the church begins.

There are several clues in the New Testament that lead one to believe that members of the early church thought that the story of the church began long before Jesus was born. In fact, they felt that the story of Jesus began long before Jesus was born. Three of the four Gospels explicitly state, each in its own way, that the story of Jesus predates his birth. By tracing Jesus' lineage back to Abraham (Matt. 1:1), Matthew seems to say that the story of Jesus cannot be understood apart from the history of Israel. In him, the whole history of Israel is fulfilled. Luke goes even farther than that. He traces the lineage of Jesus back to Adam (Luke 3:38), as if to say that in Jesus all human history is fulfilled. John, as previously noted, identifies Jesus with the Word who in the beginning was with God and was God. Other New Testament writers drop similar clues. The author of Ephesians suggests that God's eternal plan, hidden for ages but now revealed in Jesus Christ, is "to gather up all things in him, things in heaven and things on earth" (Eph. 1:10). It is as if the author were trying to say that God had Christ in mind when God created the world, that in Christ we see what we were meant to be, that the church expresses God's will for the whole creation from "before the foundation of the world" (Eph. 1:4).

These New Testament clues for identifying where the story of the church begins led Martin Luther to believe that "the holy Christian Church is the principal work of God, for the sake of which all things were made."[2] They led John Calvin to think of the church as a living organism that evolved through the centuries. Calvin saw in Adam and Eve the church in embryo, which fetally developed under the patriarchs, was born at the exodus, and has Abraham as its father. From its embryonic state on, according to Calvin, the church might be compared to a human organism, pressing toward its goal, not without setbacks to be sure, but constantly being born again.[3] According to both Luther and Calvin, the story of the church begins at creation.

Reformed Christians have always been prolific composers of creeds. No one creed has ever been given supreme authority in the Reformed tradition. The Bible is the supreme authority. But the creeds that were written by Reformed people indicate how those people read and interpreted the Bible. Therefore, it may be instructive to take our question of where the story of the church begins to representative samples of Reformed creeds. When we read the creeds of the Reformed tradition, all of which were intended as catholic rather than sectarian statements of faith, we see that the church is defined in the same broad and inclusive terms as those used by Luther and Calvin. The Heidelberg Catechism (1563), composed in Germany, had great influence on the life and mind of Reformed churches in Hungary, the Netherlands, and the United States. It states that "out of the whole human race, from the beginning to the end of the world, the Son of God, by his Spirit and Word, gathers, defends, and preserves for himself unto everlasting life, a chosen communion in the unity of the true faith."[4] The Belgic Confession (1561), prepared by Guy de Bray, was a strong Calvinistic document and became the standard of the Dutch Reformed Church. It also affirms that the church "hath been from the beginning of the world."[5] But it is the Scots Confession (1560), which was composed within the space of four days by John Knox and was the finest document of the Scottish Reformation, that most clearly answers the question of where the story of the church begins from a Reformed point of view.

We most surely believe that God preserved, instructed, multiplied, honored, adorned, and called from death to life his Kirk in all ages since Adam until the coming of Christ Jesus in the flesh. For he called Abraham from his father's country, instructed him, and multiplied his seed; he marvelously preserved him, and more marvelously delivered his seed from the bondage and tyranny of Pharaoh; to them he gave his laws, constitutions, and ceremonies; to them he gave the land of Canaan; after he had given them judges, and afterwards Saul, he gave David to be king, to whom he gave promise that of the fruit of his loins should one sit forever upon his royal throne. To this same people from time to time he sent prophets, to recall them to the right way of their God, from which sometimes they strayed by idolatry. And although, because of their stubborn contempt for righteousness he was compelled to give them into the hands of their enemies, as had previously been threatened by the mouth of Moses, so that the holy city was destroyed, the temple burned with fire, and the whole land desolate for seventy years, yet in mercy he restored them again to Jerusalem, where the city and temple were rebuilt, and they endured against all temptations and assaults of Satan till the Messiah came according to the promise. [6]

The church, in other words, is the people of God, the community of believers, which has existed from the beginning of time. That is where the story begins.

Now what does that mean? What does it mean for contemporary faith and life to believe that the story of the church begins at creation? First, it means that the church exists as a consequence of the divine initiative. Apart from God's will and work the church would not exist at all. The denomination of which I am a part cannot possibly be understood simply by tracing its historical roots back to the Swiss Reformation, or to the first-century church, or to the experience of Israel, or even to the garden of Eden! In order to understand the church, its existence and its historical life must be traced back to the work and will of God "in the beginning." God is the founder and the foundation of the church, not human activity or experience. The church is not an end in itself but the creation and instrument of God's creative Word and empowering Spirit.

Second, to affirm that the story of the church begins at creation means that the God who creates the church is also the guarantor of its existence. It means that we neither need to fear for the future of the church nor feel that its outcome depends on us. We are called to faithfulness: to worship God, to live together as God's people, and to serve God's purposes in the world. The future of the church is in God's hands, not our own. God has never been without witnesses since the beginning of time, and it will be so until the end.

Third, to believe that the story of the church begins at creation means that there is always more to the church than the eye can see. What the eye can see is not unimportant, but it can often obscure what the eye cannot see. The organization can reject people whom God accepts and treat people in unloving and unjust ways. But, imperfect as it is, the church remains God's creation and God's instrument. The church is a strange, mixed body, which God has willed to use for God's own glory. That inexplicable and unmerited promise ought to set people free to share the church's joys and to accept the church's limitations without falling victim to utopianism on the one hand or cynicism on the other.

Finally, to trace the story of the church to the very beginning of God's creating underscores the fact that the mission of the church is to the whole inhabited world. From the very beginning, God created humankind for fellowship with God and each other. The whole inhabited earth was to be God's church, a people in fellowship with God and with one another. God's intention for the world was not fulfilled. Men and women rebelled. The harmony for which people, families, governments, economies, and cultures were made was destroyed. If God's purposes were to be accomplished, something had to be done. "The deliverance of the Church from its commencement down to the coming of Christ," Calvin said, "might be called a renewal of the world [*ûn renouvellement incroyable, qu seconde creation du monde*]."[7] It is to the story of this unparalleled renewal or renovation of the world, the story of the church as harbinger of the new creation, that we now turn.

GOD'S UNPARALLELED
RENOVATION OF THE WORLD

The Bible tells the story of God, the story of God's loving plan and of human misbehavior, and of God's unparalleled renovation of the world. In so doing, the Bible tells the story of the church. We cannot tell the whole story here, but we can recall it in bare outline in order to be reminded of what the church is and is to be about, and who we are as members of it.

In the beginning, God created a world of order and purpose by God's Word and Spirit. God created the natural world to be a world of order and purpose. God formed it out of nothing, or out of sheer chaos, by the power of God's Word. Nature is independent of God in the sense that it is not God, but it derives its existence from, is responsive to, and remains dependent upon God. God gave to nature its life in order that nature might serve God's purposes for the world. Calvin used bread to illustrate this point.[8] There is no strength in bread to nourish us, for we do not live by bread alone. We live by "the hidden grace of God" or the "secret power of God," in Calvin's language, whereby God gives to bread the energy to nourish us. God created nature for peace, harmony, love, and community, according to God's will. Nature was ordained to minister to the human spirit.

God also created humankind as two, man and woman, and intended that together they should live an ordered and purposeful existence. God created them free and responsible, giving to them the capacity to reason and the ability to love. By this same creative Spirit, God gave them life by breathing life into them. God made them creative in God's own image and equipped them for social and cultural life. God willed that men and women should live together in love, justice, and peace, giving them relational and political skills, possibilities, and opportunities, that they might organize their life together. They were asked to till the earth, to build a society, to exercise dominion over the earth as stewards as well as heirs of the grace of life. Sometimes we read the book of Genesis and interpret creation as something that happened a long time ago. That it did. God created "in the beginning," but the Christian doctrine of creation also denotes the continuing creativity of God. God continues to create and to recreate the world: nature, men and women, and societies as well.

Anyone who reads past the second chapter of Genesis, however, knows that something happened to God's creation that marred and distorted it almost beyond recognition. Men and women apparently were not satisfied with the divine arrangement of things. They were unwilling to live as creatures subordinate to the will of the Creator. They wanted to be gods themselves. They rebelled against their Creator, refusing to live as God wanted them to live, and attempted to live after their own devices instead. They sought their own gain and pleasure rather than God's will, and the consequences were nothing short of disastrous. They perverted and exploited the world of nature. They lost contact with the will of God for their lives. They turned against one another, lied, cheated, stole, and killed for personal advantage. In fact, they lost the capacity to live with each other in love, justice, and peace. They were expelled from God's garden or kingdom and were forced to live in a world that had fallen from the heights of the divine plan and purpose. Self-interest rather than the common good became both the end and the means of human behavior. Personal and social chaos reigned.

Christians call this distortion of God's creation "the fall." Like creation, the fall is not only something that happened long ago. It did happen long ago, but it continues to happen in the life of nature, individuals, and societies today. In other words, when the Bible tells the story of God's good creation and our fallen world, it tells the story of our lives. When we read the newspaper and learn of what people are doing to each other, we are reading the contemporary details of creation and fall. When we look at our own lives and see how short we have fallen from the person God intended us to be, we are seeing the reenactment of creation and fall in ourselves. Dirty air, polluted streams and rivers, vast expanses of concrete and steel, all testify to creation and fall in contemporary life. If there were no God, or if God did not care what happened in and to the world of God's creating, there would be no hope at all for nature, people, and societies. The Bible, however, speaks of a living God and our living hope when it tells the story of the church.

The original order and purpose of God for nature, human existence, and social and political relationships were not totally destroyed by human sin and willfulness. But they were distorted almost beyond recognition, such that neither nature, nor human beings, nor human communities could ever recover their lost order and purpose by themselves. Only the God who made them could save nature, men and women, and social orders from their disaster. To that end and for that purpose, God created the church, calling it into being out of nothing even as God had created the world. According to Calvin, "The creation of the world would serve no purpose if there were no people to call upon God."[9] The order and purpose of creation are only partially restored in the church, for the church itself is part of the fallen creation. But the story of the church bears witness to, and in fact is, the ongoing story of God's renovating, renewing, and restoring activity in the world.

The story of the church as a self-conscious people of God begins to unfold with God's call of Abraham. God called Abraham and made a covenant with him and with his descendants. Abraham is not asked to renovate the fallen world. He is simply asked to trust and obey God. The promise made to Abraham is that God will use his faith and obedience as an instrument of blessing for generations yet to come. Prior to Abraham, Calvin said, the whole world was the same. "But as soon as it was said, 'I will be a God to thee and to thy seed after thee,' the Church was separated from other nations; just as in the creation of the world, the light emerged out of the darkness."[10]

The idea that God elected one person over another, and one nation instead of another, has always been repugnant to the liberal mind. It seems strange if not unfair, and the Bible does not pretend to say why God does things this way. It does say that God did not elect Abraham and his descendants because they were the most numerous or the most moral people on earth. "It was not because you were more numerous than any other people that the LORD set his heart on you and chose you. . . . It was because the LORD loved you" (Deut. 7:7–8). God chose this people simply because God loved them. They were not worthy, but God loved them. They would fail God time and time again, but God would never fail them. God chose this people not because they had a claim on God but because God had a claim on them—not for special privilege but for service. The Bible calls this claim "the covenant."

A covenant is a contract or a compact between two parties. In a covenant relationship, two parties pledge themselves to each other, each promising loyalty to the other. Some covenants are made between equal parties. The covenant of God with Abraham, however, was a covenant between unequal parties. God was Creator and Ruler of the world; Abraham and his descendants were fallen creatures living in a fallen world. God needed nothing from them; Abraham and his descendants needed everything from God. God had a mind to renovate the fallen world. For that purpose, God chose Abraham and his descendants, saying, "So shall you be my people, and I will be your God" (Jer. 11:4).

The covenant between God and this people was reestablished at Mount Sinai. Things had not gone well; the people had broken covenant with God. In most covenental agreements, when one side breaks the constituting promises, the other side is released from any continuing obligation. It was not the first time. The people had broken their promises time and time again. They had put together a history of adventure and intrigue that would rival any modern novel, from Abraham's giving of his wife into a king's bed (Gen. 20) to the murder of an Egyptian man by Moses (Exod. 2). Again and again, the people proved to be faithless. Again and again, God proved to be faithful. This is perhaps the main theme of the Bible, and thus the basis of the church's faith and hope: the faithlessness of God's people and the faithfulness of God.

When this people were in Egyptian bondage, God delivered them. Their exodus from Egypt was surrounded by miracle and mystery, and no one knows exactly what happened. Perhaps it is just as well. "Mysteries are the food of the mind and all the fundamental mysteries are necessary to sanity," said I. A. Richards, the great philosopher of the twentieth century, who felt a certain familiarity with the incomprehensible. "In asylums you meet people who have the answers; sane people never have the answers."[11] The Bible does not pretend to have all the answers. It simply says that whatever happened, however it came to pass, God delivered this people from the land of bondage. God delivered them for a purpose, just as God had called Abraham for a purpose, and the purpose was still the same. By this deliverance God would reestablish this people to be God's instrument in the unparalleled renovation of a fallen world.

God made a new covenant with Israel, choosing them again and anew, asking only that they should have no other god. God gave them law as an expression of God's commitment to them. The law was not given to threaten the people, nor did God require obedience to the law as a precondition for the divine favor. The law was an expression of the original order and purpose for which God created nature, human beings, and societies in the beginning. In obeying the law, the people would fulfill their creation. They would live as God meant for them to live when they were conceived. In so being and living, they would serve as God's instrument for the renovation of the world.

The story of Israel, told in the Old Testament, includes various and sundry events and characters, but the motif of the story remains the same throughout: the faithlessness of God's people and the faithfulness of God. God gave to Israel kings to lead the people in faith and service. Saul, David, and Solomon were the three that were best remembered and most revered, but even they failed to live up to the expectations with which they were anointed. Neither the people nor the kings kept their covenant with God. Soon it became evident that Israel would not and could not live up to its high calling. The prophets spoke of God's judgment and called Israel to repent, but theirs was no counsel of despair. The prophet's word was God's call to Israel to trust the faithfulness of God. Jeremiah looked forward to a new covenant based not on laws but written upon the hearts of the people. This new covenant would be established on forgiveness: "No longer shall they teach one another, or say to each other, 'Know the LORD,' for they shall all know me, from the least of them to the greatest, says the LORD; for I will forgive their iniquity, and remember their sin no more" (Jer. 31:34).

Ezekiel lamented over Israel. He envisioned Israel as sheep that had been scattered abroad (34:12) and as dry bones (37:1–14). Yet, like Jeremiah, his was not a counsel of despair. Ezekiel knew that God cared for this flock like a shepherd and that, by the power of the Spirit, God would make the dry bones live. There developed the idea of a "remnant," God's faithful few, who "shall stand as a signal to the peoples" (Isa. 11:10) and show forth "the plan that is planned concerning the whole earth" (Isa. 14:26). The nation may be in exile, but "a remnant will return" (Isa. 10:21), and God's will and work will be done through them. Later, Isaiah understood the existence and task of God's people in terms of a servant who suffers for other people (chaps. 42, 53). The Suffering Servant would bear the punishment that rightly belonged to others, taking their guilt on himself. The Suffering Servant would bear the sin of many, even as God must bear it, and offer God's forgiveness to all. The Suffering Servant also would convene a people who would be God's servants. They too would bear the sin and guilt of others and announce God's forgiveness to all. God covenanted with this people that the world would be renovated and that they would be the instrument of that renovation.

> So shall my word be that goes out from my mouth;
>   it shall not return to me empty,
> but it shall accomplish that which I purpose,
>   and suceed in the thing for which I sent it.
>
> (Isa. 55:11)

The story of the church has sometimes been thought of as an hourglass lying on its side. At one time, the people of God were many in number, but progressively it was narrowed down from the nation as a whole to a few, and finally to one man, Jesus of Nazareth. Then the size of the people of God began to increase again, and shall increase, until every knee shall bow "in heaven and on earth and under the earth, and every tongue confess that Jesus Christ is Lord, to the glory of God the Father" (Phil. 2:10–11). Israel failed to be the people that God wanted them to be. They failed so miserably that God had to act again in order to facilitate a new exodus from the bondage of sin and death.

The Christian church today must be very careful to specify what it means when it says that Israel failed. The Israel of the Old Testament cannot be identified simply with the Jews of today or with the modern state of Israel. To say that Israel failed is no credit to the church. The failure of Israel is not the backdrop for the success story of the church. The failure of Israel is no excuse for the sin of anti-Semitism. When Christians speak of the failure of Israel, they speak of their own failure, the failure of the church! The story of the church, as we have seen, does not begin after the failure of Israel but at creation with Adam and Eve. The story of Israel is the story of the church, the theme of which has been repeated over and over again: the faithlessness of God's people and the faithfulness of God. A promising God refuses to give up on an unpromising people simply because God loves them and has something for them to do.

Christians believe that Jesus Christ is God's final and definitive response to the sin and fall of Adam and Eve, and to the failure of Israel and the church. His life, death, and resurrection mark God's new beginning with the world. Christians have tried to describe this new beginning in many ways. Sometimes they called Jesus Christ God's new creation. He was understood as the Second Adam. Just as God began the world with one man, so now in this one man, God begins again with creation. Jesus is the first fruit, the pioneer of our salvation. He was and did what God intended all people to be and to do. When we identify with Christ and follow him in the midst of the fallen world, we are drawn into the form and structure of existence that God intended in the beginning and that God even now is bringing to its end.

Sometimes Christians describe God's new beginning with the world in Jesus Christ as the new exodus, as though Jesus were a second Moses, the leader of people from bondage to freedom. Just as the Hebrews had been delivered from the bondage of slavery by a liberating act of God at the Red Sea, so all people now have been delivered from the bondage of sin and death by the liberating act of God in Jesus Christ. This Christ event, often called the incarnation, God's becoming flesh and dwelling among us, did not do away with the old creation. Sin and death yet remain. The incarnation did not solve the problems of living on God's terms in the midst of a world that functions as if there were no God at all. In fact, Christ creates problems for the believer that are unknown to the unbeliever. But in him God did make a new beginning in and with the fallen world. He completed and fulfilled the creation. He completed and fulfilled the history of Israel. In him and by him, God's intention for creation was completely and perfectly realized in time and space. Jesus Christ is the self-revelation of God, in whom we encounter "the mystery of [God's] will" (Eph. 1:9).

What happened to the church? In Jesus Christ, the people of God were renewed, redefined, reorganized, and sent out into the world to bear witness to the good news of all that God had done and is doing to reverse the effects of the fall. At his baptism, Jesus consciously and publicly identified himself with the mission of the people of God. He chose the Twelve to carry forward the twelve-tribe structure of ancient Israel into a new and explosive future that was to involve the entire inhabited world. In Jesus Christ, Christians believe, God established a new covenant in and by which God's relationship with creation was renewed. Jesus did not destroy the covenant with Israel. He radicalized the covenant. A new radicalism of love, summarized in the Sermon on the Mount and demonstrated on the cross, reinterpreted the ancient law of Israel in fresh and clarifying ways.

Christians long have known that the church of Jesus Christ is dependent upon its continuity with Israel, but with no clear insight as to how the church fits into the whole scheme of things. Paul took a stab at it and promised that finally Israel would be included in the triumph of God. Few contemporary voices offer as much help. Rabbi Franz Rosenzweig was an exception. He helped Christians to understand the story of the church by suggesting that Christianity is the missionary arm of Israel. The Gentile would come to faith in the one God only through Christianity. Likewise, Will Herberg, another Jewish thinker, suggested that Christianity is Judaism's apostle. In Christianity, God opened the covenant to the whole of humankind without supplanting or superseding the covenant with the Jews. The task of the Jew is to witness to God's activity through the covenant into which the Jew entered by birth. The task of the Christian is to go into all the world and bring others into the covenant by adoption. The difference between the two is one of vocation.[12]

In the death of Jesus on the cross, the extent of God's love was revealed. Jesus on the cross was God's Suffering Servant. He bore the brunt of our sin, revealed God's forgiveness, and effected our restoration to fellowship with God. On the cross, we look deep into the heart of God, where we see God's indomitable love for people. But this is not all. Something earthshaking happened on Calvary that changed everything that once was. God accomplished something decisive in the cross of Jesus Christ that spelled the doom of sin and evil. When we try to say precisely what God did to save us in the cross of Jesus Christ, however, we soon realize that we confront a great mystery of love and suffering, justice and reconciliation, the depth of which is beyond our ken to calculate and chronicle precisely. Even though "the crucifixion of Jesus set men thinking more than anything else that has ever happened in the life of the human race,"[13] all human thoughts combined cannot fathom the mystery of God's love for people. Whatever theories we use to try to explain how God answered sin and saved us by the cross of Christ, our intent is to acknowledge that sin causes pain and that forgiveness requires the bearing of pain. The person sinned against always bears the pain. The person who commits sin, particularly when he or she realizes it as sin, also bears the pain. In fact, "the wages of sin is death" (Rom. 6:23). The one who forgives sin must pay a painful price if the power of sin is to be broken and the effects of sin relativized. In one way or another, the church has tried to say that on the cross God in Christ paid the painful price for our sin. In some mysterious but very real way, Christ stood in our stead, suffered the consequences of our sin, paid the wages that we owe, and became the instrument of our forgiveness and reconciliation with God. We do not fully understand God's great love for us, but we do believe that "in Christ God was reconciling the world to himself" (2 Cor. 5:19).

In the resurrection of Jesus from the dead, the worst deed that humankind has ever done was transformed into the very best deed that God could ever do. On Friday, human beings did their worst. We killed God's only begotten Son, but God used that dastardly deed for good. God used that heinous deed for our salvation, so that now, when we think back on the cross, we think not of the triumph of sin but of the incredible power of God's love. The cross could not stand as God's last word. Regardless of its creative possibilities, death in and of itself bears no hope for life eternal. Yet another word had to be said. The resurrection of Jesus from the dead was God's Word concerning sin and death. In the resurrection of Jesus, God demonstrated God's sovereign power over sin and death, and over the schemes of men and women as well. The resurrection of Jesus says "No!" to sin and death, and to men and women who work their sinful and dying ways in the world. The resurrection of Jesus from the dead says "Yes!" to Jesus Christ, to his way, and to all who trust and obey him. Easter showed men and women what had been going on in what had been happening since the beginning of time. A living God, who loved people and who had something in mind for people to be and do, had long been at work renovating a fallen world. For this reason, the first Christians called the Christ event "gospel," good news, and understood their task to be one of sharing this gospel with the whole inhabited world.

When we understand the church in the context of the whole story of God's unparalleled renovation of the fallen world, we gain a new perspective on its routine, sometime petty, and often boring institutional life. We gain insight into the meaning of membership in the church that goes much deeper than any local or parochial definition. We see that in its local, denominational, and ecumenical expression, the church is more than the eye can see. We understand that the church is the people of God, created, elected, rescued, and restored by God, and called to be God's instrument for the renovation of the world. To be a member of the church, therefore, is not simply to belong to another worthwhile institution in town. It is to be given a place and a part, and it is to take one's place and play one's part in the most exciting, demanding, and important enterprise in the world. It is to be joined with our Creator and Redeemer in the task of renovating the world.

Chapter 4

The Christian Community

All saints that are united to Jesus Christ their head, by his Spirit and by faith, have fellowship with him in his graces, sufferings, death, resurrection, and glory; and, being united to one another in love, they have communion in each other's gifts and graces; and are obliged to the performance of such duties, public and private, as do conduce to their mutual good, both in the inward and outward man. Saints, by profession, are bound to maintain an holy fellowship and communion, in the worship of God, and in performing such other spiritual services as tend to their mutual edification; as also in relieving each other in outward things, according to their several abilities and necessities. Which communion, as God offereth opportunity, is to be extended unto all those who, in every place, call upon the name of the Lord Jesus.

Westminster Confession of Faith

The church is people who believe in God and worship God in gathered congregations. However, many people who believe in God do not worship regularly on Sunday. Sunday is their day for rest and recreation. It is a day for travel, family fun, reading a good book, or watching television. Many Christians feel that the church is not really necessary for their Christian lives. They may belong to a church, but their participation is marginal and erratic. Some even claim that they feel closer to God on the golf course or walking alone in the woods than they do in church. A Gallup poll of American religious attitudes asked: Do you think that a person can be a good Christian if he or she does not attend church? Eighty-eight percent of the unchurched respondents and 70 percent of the churched responded in the affirmative.[1] After all, is not being Christian simply a matter of believing in the existence of a Supreme Being and trying to live a good life? If that is what being Christian is about, perhaps we should dispense with the church altogether, or at least concede that it is optional, good for some but not necessary for all who identify themselves as Christian.

IS THE CHURCH NECESSARY?

John Calvin, in his *Institutes of the Christian Religion*, began his discussion of the church with the question of its necessity. Calvin may have known that only those who understood the necessity of the church in Christian faith and life could be expected to care about its doctrine, order, and practice. However that may be, Calvin was convinced that the church is necessary for the Christian life. He knew how difficult it is to be and to remain Christian with any degree of consistency, to say nothing of the difficulty of growing in one's Christian faith and life, when one tries to do these things alone. Human nature is incredibly fickle. People quickly lose interest, become bored, run out of energy, and flit from one commitment or object of loyalty to another. Their enthusiasm for the church tends to sag when year after year they are bombarded by problems, pressures, physical handicaps, and mental torments. Calvin must have known that people need help if they are to be and remain Christian, and he was convinced that God provides for us in this regard. In fact, Calvin was awed by the fact that the eternal God had stooped so low as to accommodate our human weakness and inadequacy: "Since, however, in our ignorance and sloth (to which I add fickleness of disposition) we need outward helps to beget and increase faith within us, and advance it to its goal, God has also added these aids that he may provide for our weakness."[2]

The title Calvin gives to his fourth book on the church in the *Institutes*, "The External Means or Aims by Which God Invites Us into the Society of Christ and Holds Us Therein," indicates in advance where he intends to go in his doctrine of the church. Calvin believed that the church is the context in which the justification and the sanctification of the Christian take place. God uses this community, its institutional structures and activities, to draw people to Jesus Christ, to help people to live with Jesus Christ, and to keep people from falling away from Jesus Christ. *Justification* and *sanctification* are two great words in our theological vocabulary to which the Protestant Reformers often referred. Since we shall refer to them either explicitly or implicitly time and time again, we do well to define them here as simply as possible.

Justification has to do with our salvation. Justification by grace through faith means that we are not saved by thinking good thoughts or by doing good works but only by the grace of God. God forgives us even though we do not deserve to be forgiven. We accept God's forgiveness by faith, which itself is a gift of God. We think good thoughts and do good works in order to express our thanksgiving to God for what God has given us. Calvin understood justification in this way: "Therefore, we explain justification simply as the acceptance with which God receives us into his favor as righteous men. And we say that it consists in the remission of sins and the imputation of Christ's righteousness."[3]

Sanctification has to do with our growth in faith and grace. We may not be getting better and better every day and in every way. Perfection is something that will always elude us in this life. Sin is ever at work in our members, as we are told by the apostle Paul, affecting our best deeds as well as our worst. We do have reason to believe, however, that we can in grow in grace and in the knowledge of God. We have every right to expect some degree of progress in our understanding of God, some degree of maturation in our Christian experience, some victories, however small, over our temptations, some deepening of our love of God and neighbor. This process of becoming is that to which sanctification refers.

Justification and sanctification constitute the one act or gift of God. Being two sides of the same coin, justification and sanctification cannot be separated from each other, only distinguished as two manifestations of God's grace. Justification, God's forgiveness of our sins, is not necessarily prior in the chronology of the Christian life. God does not first justify us and then begin to sanctify us. In fact, Calvin discussed sanctification before justification, because sanctification is often the context in which men and women hear the gospel and repent of their sins. Sanctification is the long process, which extends over an entire lifetime, whereby God stoops to our weakness by providing "the external means or aims" necessary to include us in the church and hold us therein.

The church, therefore, is the context of God's justifying and sanctifying activity, in which men and women are included, nurtured, and held in God's forgiving grace. The church is God's gift to us, God's provision for our weakness, God's accommodation to our need, whereby God gives us the aids and helps we need in order to be and to stay Christian in the world. Calvin thought of the church in parental terms, drawing on the ideas of Cyprian, who said in the third century, "You cannot have God for your Father unless you have the Church for your Mother."[4] Calvin referred to the church as the Mother of the faithful, believing that God graciously gathers men and women into the church in order that God might nourish and sustain them in their Christian faith and life, even as a mother nourishes and sustains her child. The church is God's renovating activity in the world, and thus it is a part of the gospel. "The gospel about Christ is also the gospel about his Church."[5]

THE TRUTH AND ERROR
OF A CARICATURE OF PROTESTANTISM

John T. McNeill noted how tragic it is that people try to be and to stay Christian alone, and how mistaken it is to caricature Protestantism as religious individualism. Reformed Christianity is neither autonomous individualism nor the license of the religious individual to go it alone. Reformed Christians share the

conviction of all Christians that, in fact, God has saved us from isolation and soli-
tariness by giving us the church. It is a caricature to describe the Protestant as one
who "pushes on from nationalism in religion to sectarianism, and from sectarianism to a religious solitude of pure private judgment freed from authority and
association."[6] So the caricature goes: the medieval church enslaved individuals to
church authority and power; the Protestant Reformation set individuals free to
be responsible for themselves and subject to no one.

There is some truth in every caricature, else it would not tempt us. First,
Protestants did stand against many elements of the medieval church, and Protestants have continued to stress the responsibility of Christian people to critique
the institutional church by saying "No" to its doctrine and practice when No
needs to be said. Protestants make a radical distinction between the ultimate and
the penultimate, between the perfection of God and the imperfection of all
human institutions. God created and loves the church, but God never completely
identifies with the church. God stands over against both the church and the
world. God is free to use the church or not to use the church, to confirm the life
and work of the church or to judge and correct it by pressures from the outside.
This means that sometimes, if the Christian is to obey God rather than people,
he or she must stand over against the church in protest.

There is a second element of truth in this caricature of Protestantism. Protestantism does affirm the importance of the individual in relation to the larger community. The role and place of the individual in Christian community will be
discussed later in terms of the priesthood of all believers. But it is worthy of note
here that Protestants, and particularly Reformed Protestants, never intended
that the individual Christian should be relegated to a position of no importance
by the group. Whatever else may be said about the primacy of the community
and the unity of the church, no group or group opinion, no party or party line,
ever has any business running roughshod over the faith and conscience of the
Christian individual. One of the preliminary principles, first drawn up by American Presbyterians in the Synod of New York and Philadelphia in 1788 and fixed
to the Form of Government, reflected the conviction of Westminster that "God
alone is lord of the conscience." This principle represents the conviction that each
individual is personally responsible before God for his or her faith and life. In the
end, every person must stand alone in the presence of Almighty God and give
account for the stewardship of life.

There is some truth, therefore, in the caricature of Protestantism as the recovery of Christian individualism, but this truth is not the whole truth. Taken out
of the context of the communal character of Christian life, Christian individualism is selfish at best, and at worst a repudiation of the gospel. Religious individualism always leads to a distortion of the Reformed doctrine of the church. The
Protestant Reformation, both in its Lutheran and Reformed traditions, sought
to recover the social and ethical reality of the church as the Christian community. The Reformed doctrine of the church begins, not with the Christian individual but with the *communio sanctorum,* the communion of saints. In their

acceptance of the Apostle's Creed, the Reformers affirmed their faith in the holy catholic church and the communion of saints, and they understood the one to be descriptive of the other.

THE CHRISTIAN KOINONIA

When did the church become more than a collection of individuals? In other words, when did the church become the church? Pentecost is often called the birthday of the church. Pentecost is not where the story of the church begins, as we have seen, for the story of God's creating and redeeming activity with people long preceded the first century. But Pentecost was the occasion of the great rebirth of the church, when the people of God were reconstituted and equipped for their mission in the world. At Pentecost, the church was empowered for action by God's Word and sent forth into the world by God's Spirit.

Acts 2 records the strange events of that day of Pentecost and interprets their meaning for the church. Pentecost was the Feast of Weeks, which, along with Passover and the Feast of Tabernacles, was one of the three great feasts of Judaism. All of the people of Israel were required to attend and all of the disciples were together in one place. Suddenly there came a sound from heaven "like the rush of a violent wind" (Acts 2:2). There appeared to them "tongues as of fire" (2:3). They were filled with the Holy Spirit and began to speak in strange tongues. Others overheard the commotion and thought that the Christians were drunk, but Peter stood up in the assembly and interpreted the event in the light of the prophet Joel:

> In the last days it will be, God declares,
> that I will pour out my Spirit upon all flesh,
>   and your sons and your daughters shall prophesy,
> and your young men shall see visions,
>   and your old men shall dream dreams.
>
> (2:17)

After this, Peter proclaimed the good news of Jesus Christ, testifying that Jesus was the fulfillment of the history of Israel. When they heard Peter's words, they were "cut to the heart" (2:37) and wondered what to do. Peter called them to repent and be baptized, and promised that they would receive the Holy Spirit: "For the promise is for you, for your children, and for all who are far away, everyone whom the Lord our God calls to him" (2:39). The author of the book of Acts records that many who heard Peter were baptized and that about three thousand people were added to the church on that day. They devoted themselves to the apostolic teaching, to fellowship, to the breaking of bread, and to prayer.

So what really happened at Pentecost? Would the rush of the mighty wind and the descent of fiery tongues have been recorded on film had someone made a video of the events of that day? We do not know, but probably not. Much of the language used in Acts 2 is picture language, the language of simile and metaphor; thus, we cannot assume that the author's intention was to give us a literal account of the events of the day. Rather, the author was drawing on the most graphic language he could find to describe the meaning of the day for the life of the church. Something overwhelming happened to the disciples of Jesus on the day of Pentecost that had a lasting effect on the church. The Holy Spirit filled people's lives. Whereas before they were a gathering of individuals with different languages and understandings, at Pentecost they both remained diverse and became one people. In addition, though diverse of person and tongue, they understood and communicated with one another. The Tower of Babel incident (Gen. 11) was turned on its head. Language became the vehicle for, not a barrier to, human community. Those who had once lived separate lives were united in and by a common spirit and a common task. There was no other way to describe the situation, except to say that they were filled with the Holy Spirit.

Who is this Holy Spirit? The story of the church depends on the answer given to that question. Our understanding of and participation in the church today will reflect how we answer that question. If the Holy Spirit, which came upon the church at Pentecost, is simply another name for the intense religious enthusiasm of those who were there, a warm and friendly feeling of fellowship and mutual belonging, then the story of the church is no more than the story of religious experience and a human institution. Intense feelings are not unique. Feelings ran high in the American Revolution. Colleagues in an exciting business enterprise often have a warm and friendly feeling for one another. Men and women were unified and understood one another in intense ways on the civil rights march from Selma to Montgomery. There have been many good, principled, tender human emotions in the history of human experience. The stories of the American Revolution, of an exciting business venture, and of the civil rights march may be told in winsome ways, but they are all human stories and not necessarily the story of God. If the Holy Spirit, on the other hand, is none other than the eternal God, Creator of the heavens and the earth, who was in Christ, then Pentecost and the subsequent history of the church tell more than a human story. They tell the story of God.

Some three centuries after Pentecost, the church still had not come to terms with the Holy Spirit. In fact, there were several different opinions about who the Holy Spirit is. The Council of Nicaea, which met in A.D. 325 to deal with the question of who Jesus Christ is in relation to God, was silent about the deity of the Holy Spirit. Scripture itself, conceded Gregory of Nazianzus, the bishop of Constantinople in the fourth century, does not "very clearly or very often write him God in express words, as it does first the Father and afterwards the Son."[7] Similarly, the liturgy of the church in those early Christian centuries did not provide instances of worship or prayer addressed to the Holy Spirit. Some people thought that the Holy Spirit was a natural, ministering spirit that people might experience when they shared their lives with each other. Others thought that the Holy Spirit participated in God's Spirit and was thus unique, but that the Spirit was less than God. According to Philip Schaff, the so-called *filioque* controversy over the Spirit's relation to the Father and the Son, next to the question of the authority of the pope, was probably the source of the greatest schism in Christendom.[8] In a remarkable summary of this controversy, Gregory of Nazianzus (A.D. 380) wrote, "Of the wise men among ourselves, some have conceived of him [the Holy Spirit] as an activity, some as a creature, some as God; and some have been uncertain which to call him. . . . And therefore they neither worship him nor treat him with dishonor, but take up a neutral position."[9]

The church moved to clarify the identity of the Holy Spirit and the Spirit's relation to the Father and the Son at the Council of Constantinople in A.D. 381. Here the Nicene faith, which fifty-six years before had affirmed the consubstantiality of the Son with the Father, was reaffirmed and applied also to the Spirit. The formula that expresses the prevailing opinion of the council is: one "ousia" in three "hypostases"—one Godhead existing simultaneously in three modes of being. The one God imparts God's being to the other two persons. God causes them, so to speak, and is them. The Son is begotten from the Father, and the Spirit proceeds. The analogy of the universal and its particulars was used to illustrate this conviction, specifically the relationship between universal human being and particular human being. Just as each individual represents universal humanity and is identified by certain characteristics that mark the individual off from all other individuals, so each of the divine hypostases is the "ousia" or essence of the Godhead marked by certain distinguishing characteristics (i.e., fatherhood, sonship, and sanctifying power). Thus, the identity of the persons in the Godhead is determined by their origin and relationship one to the other. The Godhead is not divided thereby, for the Father never acts independently of the Son, nor the Son of the Spirit. "The divine action begins from the Father, proceeds through the Son, and is completed in the Holy Spirit; none of the Persons possesses a separate operation of His own, but one identical energy passes through all Three."[10] It was the conviction of the church, stated at Constantinople, that the Holy Spirit is the Spirit of Jesus Christ, and thus of God.

It was Augustine, however, who gave the mature and final clarification to the identity of the Holy Spirit. One of the ways he did so was to explain what the procession of the Spirit is and means, and how it differs from the generation of the Son. Augustine taught the doctrine of the double procession of the Spirit from the Father and the Son. The Greek church held that the Holy Spirit proceeds, or originates, from the Father (*ex Patre procedentum*). Augustine, the Latin church, and later the Reformed churches held that the Holy Spirit proceeds from the Father and the Son (*ex Patre Filioque procedit*). Considerable controversy centered around the word *filioque,* which means "and the Son."

What did this controversy have to do with the doctrine of the church? Both points of view identified the Holy Spirit with God. Both points of view distinguished the Holy Spirit from the Son. The difference, according to Latin critics, was that in the Greek view—that the Spirit proceeds from the Father—the assumption is that God is revealed to people directly and without identifying mediation. God may be known in nature, in spiritual experience, or in intimate human relationships, apart from Jesus Christ. The Latin view, that the Spirit proceeds from the Father and the Son, sought to affirm the particularity of God's revelation in Jesus Christ. History and not nature, in other words, is the key to what God is doing in the world. The Spirit who is present and active in the world today is not just any spirit but the Spirit of God revealed and defined in the life, death, and resurrection of Jesus Christ. Furthermore, the Latin view suggests that in revelation, as in the Godhead, there is communion.[11] To say that the Holy Spirit proceeds from the Father and the Son is to affirm that there is communion in the Godhead between the Father and the Son, and that the Spirit that comes to us from the Father and the Son is the Spirit of love. The Father loves the Son and the Son loves the Father. The Spirit that proceeds from such love is none other than the Spirit of community. The story of the church, therefore, is more than the story of a human institution. It is the continuing story of the love of God at work in the world, drawing people together by the Holy Spirit, and making of them a Christian community after the being and nature of God.

Jesus Christ was not physically present with the early Christian church. Nevertheless, the first Christians had a sense of his real presence in their midst through the presence of the Holy Spirit. The word often used in the New Testament to describe this sense of presence that bound men and women together in common faith and life is *koinonia*. The word is a transliteration of a Greek word for which no English word is an adequate translation. *Koinonia* is often translated as "fellowship" or "community," but neither is adequate to carry the intended meaning. In the New Testament, *koinonia* is used for the intimate relationship that Christians have with God (1 John 1:3), with Jesus Christ (1 John 1:3; Phil. 3:10), with the Spirit (Phil. 2:1), with the mystery of God's plan hidden for ages (Eph. 3:9), with the gospel (Phil. 1:5), with the mission of the church (2 Cor. 8:4), and with others in the church (Acts 2:42; 1 John 1:3). The word points to the fact that those upon whom the Holy Spirit descended at Pentecost were drawn into a common life and ministry by a common gospel, rooted and grounded in a common relationship to the triune God. They entered into this koinonia by repentance and baptism to demonstrate that this association was something brand new. The Christian koinonia had continuity with the past. The first Christians claimed the history of Israel as their heritage, but they nevertheless were convinced that Christian community represented a new act of God in accordance with the promise of the risen Christ and in fulfillment of ancient prophecy. Paul Lehmann described the koinonia as "the fellowship creating reality of Christ's presence in the world,"[12] and thus God's renovating activity in the world.

At the organizational center of the early Christian koinonia was a group of people who had been in close fellowship with Jesus before the crucifixion and who taught others about Jesus. Members of the koinonia broke bread together as Jesus had done with his disciples before his passion and after the resurrection. They also prayed together. It has been suggested that the prayers of the early church were a means by which the continuity with the history of Israel was maintained and celebrated. The prayers were likely temple prayers taken from the liturgies of ancient Israel, indicating that "the new fellowship was born in the matrix of an older community, the old Israel."[13] Furthermore, they "had all things in common" (*koina*). They sold their goods and possessions and distributed them as any had need (Acts 2:45), indicating that, for a time at least, a community of material goods was practiced. Perhaps this in itself is powerful testimony to the overwhelming reality of Christ's presence felt by members of the early church through the Holy Spirit. It was material manifestation of the fact that, in Christ, these men and women knew themselves as having been given to each other in order that they might live with and for each other as people of one heart and soul. Apparently this practice of having all things in common changed before too long. We do not know why. The relationship of Christians to economics has changed time and again ever since. Money and possessions have always posed a challenge, if not a threat, to Christian community. "But there is a deep unchanging sense in which Christians have 'all things common' here and hereafter,"[14] that the call of Christ to discipleship involves men and women in a community of shared faith and life. This conviction has continued to find expression in the church in one way or another generation after generation.

In summary, three things are worth noting concerning the early Christian church. First, the Christian church experienced its rise not in isolated individual experience but in the Christian koinonia of those who shared a profound and transforming experience of Jesus Christ. The chief function of the early Christian community was to interpret that experience in terms of social living, to extend the number of those who shared it, and to perpetuate it in future generations.[15] Second, the Christian koinonia was understood as a new act of God, even though it was continuous and consistent with God's prior acts in the history of Israel. God's mind had not changed, nor had God forsaken the chosen people. God had elected to make known the mystery that had been hidden for ages, namely, that the Gentile as well as the Jew was included in the promise, that all people are members of God's one human family and thus joint heirs of God's unparalleled renovation of the world. Third, the Christian koinonia was to be the context of interrelatedness in which men and women would grow into "real maturity—that measure of development which is meant by 'the fulness of Christ'" (Eph. 4:13 PHILLIPS).

Growth into real maturity was never understood by those first Christians simply as individual growth, much less as self-development or self-fulfillment. It was always a matter of community growth, in the context of which the individual grew and matured. The image of the body was particularly suggestive. No part of the body grows apart from the rest, else the body is distorted. Christian growth is a matter of each part of the body functioning properly, with each part related to the other and the whole body related to Christ, so that the growth of one into real maturity occurs only with the growth of all. According to Paul Lehmann, "What psychology knows as the problem of integration, what sociology knows as the problem of community, Christian faith discerns and delineates as the problem of the head and the body. . . . Maturity is the integrity in and through interrelatedness which makes it possible for each individual member of an organic whole to be himself in togetherness, and in togetherness each to be himself."[16] It was in the Christian koinonia that men and women were drawn into an intimate relationship with God. It was in the Christian koinonia that these same men and women were understood, accepted, respected, and befriended. Here they came to their deepest and freest self-realization, not through analysis or therapy but in the exchange of life and mutual service. Koinonia was experienced as the gracious gift of God to people, their inclusion in what God was doing to renovate the world, a laboratory of humanization.

> Here is a laboratory of maturity in which, by the operative (real) presence and power of the Messiah-Redeemer in the midst of his people, and through them of all people, the will to power is broken and displaced by the power to will what God wills. The power to will what God wills is the power to be what man has been created and purposed to be. It is the power to be and to stay human, that is, to attain wholeness or maturity. For maturity is the full development in a human being of the power to be truly and fully himself in being related to others who also have the power to be truly and fully themselves. The Christian koinonia is the foretaste and the sign in the world that God has always been and is contemporaneously doing what it takes to make and to keep human life human. This is the will of God "as it was in the beginning, is now, and ever shall be, world without end."[17]

THE COMMUNION OF SAINTS

If the Christian koinonia, the fellowship or community of men and women in and with Christ, was the normative experience of God's will and work for the early church, the development of the idea of the communion of saints gave to that experience its formal expression. We are not always comfortable with the word *saint* today. It smacks of a perfection in spiritual things to which most human beings do not attain.

The word *saint,* however, means something quite different in the Bible and in the history of the church. A saint is not a perfect person by any means. Some saints may well live more moral lives than others and some may be genuinely pious people, but neither morality nor piety makes or breaks a saint. The word *saint* in the New Testament refers to ordinary men and women in a particular time and place (Rome, Corinth, Ephesus) whose only distinction is that they have been chosen by God, claimed by Jesus Christ, and convened by the Holy Spirit to be the church. Paul's letter to the church in Rome is addressed to "all God's beloved in Rome, who are called to be saints" (Rom. 1:7). The letter to the church in Philippi is addressed to "all the saints in Christ Jesus who are in Philippi" (Phil. 1:1), and it concludes with the comforting assurance that "all the saints greet you, especially those of the emperor's household" (4:22). It may help us to understand the meaning of the word *saint* if we contemplate what it means that there were saints in Caesar's household! Saints are ordinary men and women, living in some particular time and place, sometimes in compromising circumstances such as Caesar's household, through whom God intends to accomplish this unparalleled renovation of the world.

We do not often use the word *saint* to refer to Christians today, but it is very likely that you and I, had we lived in the early Christian centuries, would have been called saints. We are the people of God in this day and time, believers in Jesus Christ and members of his church, as they were then. Chances are we are not much better or worse than those to whom Paul wrote his several letters. Thus, in spite of the fact that the word comes from the Latin *sanctus,* which means "holy," we are not excluded. Christians are saints, holy men and women, for three reasons. First, Christians are saints, not because they are holy but because God is holy. Christians are saints because, the holy God has chosen to identify with them. Second, Christians are saints because, as believers in Jesus Christ and as members of his church, they are involved in a process of growth or sanctification in the things that pertain to God. Third, Christians are saints because God has called them out and set them apart for a particular task or function in God's plan to renovate the fallen world. The word *holy,* as we shall see more clearly in the next chapter, also means "set apart" or "different." God has always chosen people, set them apart and differentiated them from all the rest, not for special privilege but for special service in God's kingdom. It is instructive to note, however, that no single individual is referred to as a saint in the New Testament, for no one is sanctified or set apart alone. A Christian is never "a 'Lone Ranger' who rides off in lonely individualism to serve God and become righteous."[18] Saints in the New Testament are found only in the plural, in the communion of saints.

Karl Barth defined the communion of saints as "a provisional representation of the new humanity in the midst of the old."[19] That definition is suggestive for our understanding of the nature and mission of the church. What is the new humanity? Christians believe that the new humanity was inaugurated in Jesus Christ. He was the Second Adam, the new creation, God's fresh start with human life in this world. Jesus Christ was the pioneer, the archetype or model, not only of our salvation but of the salvation of all people. He was what God wills all people to be. You and I are not like him now. We live in between two great events: the inauguration of the new humanity in Jesus Christ and the final manifestation of the new humanity in his coming again. In between these two great events—the first and second advent of Jesus Christ—the church lives as the communion of saints, the holy community of God's people in the intervening period, the congregation of ordinary men and women whose only claim to fame is that they know the new humanity in fact as well as in faith and are willing to bear witness to it in the midst of the fallen world. The witness of the church to the new humanity inaugurated by God in Jesus Christ is always a provisional representation because it is always imperfect and partial. It is a provisional representation because the church, like all men and women, is in between and on the way, in between those two great events, on the way from the advent of Jesus Christ to the fulfillment of God's will and work. The communion of saints is a provisional representation of the new humanity in the midst of the old, a light in the darkness, ordinary men and women whom God has claimed and called to be God's instrument in the unparalleled renovation of the world.

When we confess our faith by means of the Apostles' Creed, we say, "I believe in . . . the communion of saints." When we say that, we do not mean that we believe in the communion of saints in the same sense that we believe in God, or in Jesus Christ, or in the Holy Spirit. We are really saying that we believe that the communion of saints exists, even though sometimes we cannot see it or do not experience it in our local churches. Sometimes the communion of saints is obscured by our sin and disobedience. Sometimes, if we are to believe the Bible, God judges us by withdrawing from us, hardening our hearts and clouding our eyes. At times, the communion of saints manifests itself to us when we least expect it. It comes to us as an event, an experience of close communion that breaks through our otherwise routine experiences, as we worship or learn or serve in the church. The communion of saints is rarely, if ever, coincident with the membership rolls of our churches. It is something for which the Christian must pray, something that always comes as a gift of God, and something for which we must be profoundly grateful.

Christians believe that the communion of saints manifests itself in two ways: as a communion among saints and as a communion in the gifts and treasures of Christ. "What do you understand by the communion of saints?" asks Question 55 of the Heidelberg Catechism. The answer follows: "First, that believers one and all, as partakers of the Lord Christ, and all his treasures and gifts, shall share in one fellowship. Second, that each one ought to know that he is obliged to use his gifts freely and with joy for the benefit and welfare of other members."[20]

Very early in the history of the church, the vision of the koinonia was expanded in response to human experience. The church had to come to terms with the fact that the world was not coming to an end as quickly as Christians initially had expected. The first generation of believers grew old and died, and children were being born to Christian parents. Something of this dilemma is reflected in the letter to the Hebrews, as the author recalls the names of some of the great biblical heroes and then says, "All of these died in faith without having received the promises, but from a distance they saw and greeted them. They confessed that they were strangers and foreigners on the earth" (Heb. 11:13). The author reflects the dilemma of the unfulfilled and incomplete life, as well as the expanded vision of the Christian community, when he adds "that they would not, apart from us, be made perfect" (11:40). The word "perfect" here means whole, complete, fulfilled. Those first Christians, in other words, had to come to terms with the fate of men and women who died in the Lord before the final completion of God's will and work. Christians believed so intensely in the reality of God's

love that it was not difficult for them to understand it as something that extends
beyond the bounds of death. They sensed a very real continuity between life with
Christ on earth and life with Christ beyond death. The veil that separated the living from the dead became very thin indeed. Jürgen Moltmann has reminded us
of a contemporary example of this early church experience of the community of
saints. In the worship of many Latin American base communities, when the
names of the "disappeared" and the martyrs are read aloud, the congregation
responds with the cry, "Presente!" They are present, and there is communion
between the living and the dead.[21] We honor this communion among saints
when we sing of "the church's one foundation":

> Yet she on earth hath union
> With God the Three in One,
> And mystic sweet communion
> With those whose rest is won.

Or, at time of death, when we sing:

> For all the saints who from their labors rest,
> Who Thee by faith before the world confessed,
> Thy name, O Jesus, be forever blest.
> Alleluia! Alleluia!

> O blest communion, fellowship divine!
> We feebly struggle, they in glory shine;
> Yet all are one in Thee, for all are Thine.
> Alleluia! Alleluia!

    The liturgy, sacraments, hymns, and confessions of faith, which Christians
share together in the life of the church, suggest the second way in which the communion of saints manifests itself, namely, as a communion in the gifts and treasures of Christ. Christians not only have "mystic sweet communion" with people
of every age and place who confess Jesus Christ as Savior and Lord. Christians
also experience communion with each other in the sharing of the acts and activities of the visible church, which are God's gifts for the upholding and upbuilding of the community. The communion of saints, in other words, is the event or
occasion in which the saints (*sancti*) participate together in sacred things (*sancta*).
    One of these gifts that Christians have communion is "the faith once deliv-
ered," those foundational convictions that regulate and correct the Christian
memory and hope. This set of convictions is often referred to as the *regula
fidei,* the rule of faith. There have always been disagreements in the church,
but Christians for the most part have agreed on what there is to disagree about:
God, Jesus Christ, the Holy Spirit, the Bible, the church. More positively, there
has developed in every century a Christian consensus concerning what the faith
of the church is. Christians may disagree at points within this consensus, but
they remain bound together by affirmations held in common. We honor this

communion in the faith of the church in many ways, but no more graphically than when we repeat a great creed, such as the Apostles' Creed or the Nicene Creed, in corporate worship.

This communion is seen most clearly, perhaps, when Christians share the sacrament of the Lord's Supper, or Communion. Since the very beginning of the Christian church, the sacrament of the Lord's Supper has been central to its life. The Lord's Supper both symbolizes and incarnates what God has done and is doing to renovate the fallen world. It actualizes who we are and who we were meant to be. Robert McAfee Brown gave us a fine illustration of the meaning of Communion out of his own experience.[22] During the Second World War, when Brown was a Navy chaplain, he celebrated the Lord's Supper in the after gun turret of a destroyer escort at sea. According to his account of the incident, there was room for only three men in the gun turret at one time. The first three to come into the gun turret to receive the bread and the wine were the white commanding officer of the ship, a white fireman's apprentice, and a black steward's mate. In the social life of the ship, of course, the three men did not mix except when duty required. At the Lord's Table, however, the three communed as one. The commanding officer, the fireman's apprentice, and the steward's mate knelt side by side in an absolute and unquestioned equality of need. In that moment, God's will was done on earth as it is in heaven. There was neither bond nor free, white nor black, officer nor enlisted man. On that sacred occasion, three human beings were in communion with God and one another. They were what God intended them to be, united with God and with each other. After the service was over, they had to rise from their knees and return to the life of the ship, where all of the old barriers to communion remained intact. But old barriers never really remain intact once Communion has been shared. To whatever extent those three men took Communion seriously, they could never again live comfortably with the divisive structures imposed upon them by the world. They had shared a foretaste, an aperitif, of what life on God's terms is and is meant to be. Once that is experienced, if only by a few, the world can never remain intact. A beachhead of the new has been established in the territory of the old. God's unparalleled renovation of the world has been proclaimed and lived in the world. A revolution has begun that will not be quelled until its end has been reached and realized.

Christians share a fellowship in many other things. They share a fellowship of need, a fellowship of forgiveness, a fellowship of hope, and a fellowship of witness to Jesus Christ in the whole inhabited world. These gifts and treasures—the Bible, the sacraments, the order and mission of the church—are not entrusted to individuals, be they clergy or laity, but to us all in conjunction with each other. The communion of saints, the communion among saints, and the communion in the gifts and treasures of Christ can never be achieved by organizational skills and management techniques. It is the gift of God to the church, the vanguard of his renovative thrust in the midst of the fallen world, which we can but receive and accept with great thanksgiving.

THE PRIESTHOOD OF ALL BELIEVERS

Thus far, we have defined the church in the Reformed tradition primarily in terms of the community, the koinonia and the communion of saints, and so it must be. The first thing that must be said about the church is that it is the people of God. It is into the church rather than to some private religious existence that individuals are saved or called, baptized, and commissioned as instruments of God's will and work. But what about the Christian individual? Is there a role or place for the individual in the Reformed doctrine of the church? The answer, of course, is yes. The life of the individual is supremely important in Reformed ecclesiology. The primary image used by the Reformers to make this point is the universal priesthood, more commonly known as the priesthood of all believers. The priesthood of all believers is "nothing less than a paraphrase of the Reformation concept of the Church."[23]

In Calvin's mind, the priesthood of all believers had to do with the access of the individual to God. Calvin believed that human sin is so grievous as to incur God's righteous curse, which bars all access to God. God as our judge has good cause for anger. Some expiation must intervene between God's just wrath and the sinful individual if the individual is ever again to have access to God. Calvin understood Christ to be the mediator between the righteous God and the sinful individual, who offered himself as the sacrifice for sin and obtained for us the access to God from which we had been barred.

> Now, Christ plays the priestly role, not only to render the Father favorable and propitious toward us by an eternal law of reconciliation, but also to receive us as his companions in this great office (Rev. 1:6). For we who are defiled in ourselves, yet are priests in him, offer ourselves and our all to God, and freely enter the heavenly sanctuary that the sacrifices of prayers and praise that we bring may be acceptable and sweet-smelling before God.[24]

It was Martin Luther, however, who gave to the universal priesthood its broadest and clearest expression. If we are to understand the meaning of priesthood in Luther's thought, we first must look more closely at the word *priest*. Many cultures and religions have had priests. Priests exist in cultures and religions in which people sense that there is something askew in their relationship with God. Priests are intermediaries between God and the people, whose function it is to try to make wrong things right. On the one hand, a priest is God's representative to the people, the one who communicates God's mind and will to them. On the other hand, a priest is the people's representative before God, the one who intercedes with God on their behalf and seeks to mend the broken relationship. In some religions, priests try to manipulate or placate God in order to influence the deity in favor of the people. This is not the case in the Bible. In the Old Testament, the priest is a servant of God's Word, who communicates God's will to people and summons them to obedience. The priest offers sacrifices to God, to be sure, but the Old Testament warns time and again against any attempt to trade with

God. The priest does not win God's favor for the people but communicates God's favor to the people, which predates all priestly activity.

In the New Testament, it is clear that the model for the idea of a priest is Jesus Christ, the great high priest.

> Since, then, we have a great high priest who has passed through the heavens, Jesus, the Son of God, let us hold fast to our confession. For we do not have a high priest who is unable to sympathize with our weaknesses, but we have one who in every respect has been tested as we are, yet without sin. Let us therefore approach the throne of grace with boldness, so that we may receive mercy and find grace to help in time of need.
>
> (Heb. 4:14–16)

Jesus Christ, our high priest, is our mediator—our only mediator both in the sense that there is none other and in the sense that we need none other—and no other priesthood is essential to us save his. He has done everything that needs to be done to restore us to a right relationship with God. He is God's representative to us, the Word made flesh. He is our representative before God, having offered no sacrifice less than himself for us and for our salvation.

What Luther did was radically to reinterpret the idea of priesthood in terms of the individual's relationship to God and neighbor. Sometimes we caricature Luther's position on the priesthood of all believers by interpreting it only in its vertical dimension, that is, each individual serving as his or her own priest, having direct access to God and needing no ordained intermediary. Luther was concerned about the individual's access to God, as was Calvin. In *The Babylonian Captivity of the Church* (1520), Luther dealt harshly with every attempt of the ecclesiastical establishment to insert a human mediator between God and the believer. Luther's own religious experience, that he, a rank sinner, had received forgiveness by simply throwing himself on the grace of God in Jesus Christ, provided him insight into the nature of the evangelical experience in general. Justification is being acquitted at the bar of justice without any merit of one's own. Grace is God's pity and compassion manifested in the forgiveness of sins and the justification of the sinner. Faith is lively, reckless confidence in the grace of God. In Luther's mind, the very essence of the Christian faith was that the believer, in faith (itself a gift of God), is able to throw himself or herself on the grace of God without any interruption or priestly mediation, and receive justification and peace. The point of it all is that the living God, revealed in Jesus Christ, is immediately accessible to the faith of the believer and that, conversely, each Christian stands naked and revealed before the face of God. But this is only one part of the doctrine of the priesthood of all believers. Luther was no rugged individualist; he was an ardent advocate of Christian community.[25]

The truth of the matter is that even when Luther spoke of the priesthood of all believers, he was speaking of the one essential ministry of the whole church. Luther was of no mind to destroy the priesthood. Luther wanted to expand the priesthood. He wanted more priests in the church, not less. Over against the medieval Catholic view, Luther stressed the priesthood of the church:

> Let every one, therefore, who knows himself to be a Christian be
> assured of this, that we are all equaly priests, that is to say, we have the
> same power in respect to the Word and the sacraments. However, no
> one may make use of this power except by the consent of the com-
> munity or by the call of a superior. (For what is the common prop-
> erty of all, no individual may arrogate to himself, unless he is called.)[26]

Luther never really sorted out the precise relationship between the priesthood
of the few and the priesthood of all. Later Lutherans spoke of it in terms of representation. The priesthood of the few was representative of the priesthood of all.
The church may not be dependent upon the ordained clergy for its existence, but
for its well-being it needs the few who are called and set apart by the laying on
of hands to the particular vocation of preaching, administering the sacraments,
teaching, and pastoral care. But the priesthood of the few must never obscure,
threaten, or usurp the priesthood of all. The former is a particularization if not a
representation of the latter. The ordained minister's vocation is to represent in
and to the community the general priesthood from which it originates. The
sacrament of the Lord's Supper is a good example. In 1533, Luther wrote,

> There our pastor, bishop, or minister in the pastoral office, rightly and
> honorably and publically called, having been previously consecrated,
> anointed, and born in baptism as a priest of Christ, goes before the
> alter. Publically and plainly he sings what Christ has ordained and insti-
> tuted in the Lord's Supper. He takes the bread and wine, gives thanks,
> distributes and gives them to the rest of us who are there and want to
> receive them. . . . Particularly we who want to receive the sacrament
> kneel beside, behind, and around him, man, woman, young, old,
> master, servant, wife, maid, parents, and children, even as God brings
> us together there, all of us true, holy priests, sanctified by Christ's
> blood, anointed by the Holy Spirit, and consecrated in baptism. . . .
> and we let our pastor say what Christ has ordained, not for himself as
> though it were for his person, but he is the mouth for all of us and we
> all speak the words with him from the heart and in faith, directed to
> the Lamb of God who is present for us and among us, and who accord-
> ing to his ordinance nourishes us with his body and blood.[27]

This idea of a representative ministry was carried over into Calvinism, where it
found logical expression in a representative form of government. The point is that
every member of the church, laity as well as clergy, is called to be a priest. Each
person, on becoming a Christian, is baptized into the priesthood. This is the role
and place of the individual in the Christian community.

Thus, when men and women are called of God to be Christians and are baptized into the church, they are drawn into this royal priesthood. God's purpose in
it all has not changed. God wills to use this priesthood, the church, as his instrument in the renovation of a fallen world: "But you are a chosen race, a royal priesthood, a holy nation, God's own people, in order that you may proclaim the
mighty acts of him who called you out of darkness into his marvelous light. Once
you were not a people, but now you are God's people" (1 Pet. 2:9–10). Christians
are called to be God's representatives to people and the people's representative

before God. Our priesthood and Jesus' priesthood are not identical. His priesthood was once and for all, and by it we are saved. But we are saved for a purpose, namely, that in his priesthood we might be given a share.

The priesthood of all believers, therefore, does not only mean that each person is his or her own priest. To be sure, each person does stand immediately and directly before God, and each must give account for the stewardship of life. But it also means that each person is his or her neighbor's priest. In very personal terms, it means that the minister is your priest and that you are the minister's priest; that you are my priest and that I am your priest; that we are God's representatives to each other and that we are each other's representatives before God. It means that we are to speak to each other about God, calling each other to repentance and faith. It means that we are to intercede before God for each other and to seek God's guidance and blessing. It means that we should try to become increasingly responsive to one another, tending each other in God's name and offering to each other practical and constructive help for Christ's sake. It means that we must never presume to be more than sinners together in God's sight and that we must live together as humble pensioners on God's mercy. Once again, the priesthood of all believers is no rugged individualism. It is a description of the role and place of the individual that emphatically declares that apart from the communion of saints the Christian life has little content or meaning.

In conclusion, it might be noted that the one word that best describes the priesthood of all believers is *service*. In Greek, the word is *diakonia,* from which we derive the word *deacon.* All too often, the office of deacon in the church is considered a secondary office, a task to which one is elected before one is entrusted with the more important task of governing the church. In some Reformed congregations, the board of deacons is a decision-making organization, whose task it is to manage the finances and to maintain the property. These tasks are very important for any congregation. They can be authentic vehicles for Christian service. But to limit the office of deacon and the function of the board of deacons to institutional maintenance projects is a contradiction of everything the church is and is called to be. The primary task of the deacon is not property but people. It is visiting and caring for the sick and the dying, the aged, the lonely, and the friendless. It is helping the poor, feeding the hungry, finding homes for the homeless, and working for justice and peace in the world. In short, the vocation of the diaconate is the service of people in need.

To be a priest one to another is to be a deacon one to another, whether one is actually elected to the office or not. It is to be God's representative to people and the people's representative before God. The priesthood of all believers is one of the ways individuals experience and share in the communion of saints. In our service to God and to one another, we bring the liturgy of the Lord's Supper to life and celebrate God's renovating activity in the world.

Chapter 5

What Makes
the Church the Church

*The notes of the true Kirk, therefore, we believe, confess, and avow
to be: first, the true preaching of the Word of God, in which God
has revealed himself to us, as the writings of the prophets and apostles declare; secondly, the right administration of the sacraments of
Christ Jesus, with which must be associated the Word and promise
of God to seal and confirm them in our hearts; and lastly, ecclesiastical discipline uprightly ministered, as God's Word prescribes,
whereby vice is repressed and virtue nourished. Then wherever
these notes are seen and continue for any time, be the number complete or not, there, beyond any doubt, is the true Kirk of Christ,
who, according to his promise, is in its midst.*

Scots Confession

People today who read the church's ancient story in the Bible and ponder the high
doctrine of the church in the thought of the Protestant Reformers may well raise
objections. Where in the world is this church of which the Bible and the Reformers speak? T. S. Eliot poked fun at the church when he compared it to a broad-
backed hippopotamus:

> The broad-backed hippopotamus
> Rests on his belly in the mud;
> Although he seems so firm to us
> He is merely flesh and blood.
> Flesh and blood is weak and frail,
> Susceptible to nervous shock;
> While the True Church can never fail
> For it is based upon a rock.

> The hippo's feeble steps may err
> In compassing material ends,
> While the True Church need never stir
> To gather in its dividends.[1]

When one looks at churches in a given city or town, they often appear as broad-backed hippopotamuses, stuck in the mud, susceptible to nervous shock, and compassing their material ends. Sometimes the communion of saints is hard to find, and few church members think of themselves as priests. Maybe the church of which the Bible and the Reformers speak is a myth, a fine dream that never really comes true, an ideal that never becomes actual in the real world. Most churches are architecturally out of date. They function like a business in many ways. They are seldom of one mind on ecclesiastical or social issues. Church members always seem to be fighting about something, usually about money or sex. The church is often closed to new knowledge and blind to new ways of living in society. Where is the church of which the Bible and the Reformers speak? How would I recognize it if I saw it?

CHURCH: A SEMANTIC PROBLEM

One thing we must face is the fact that we have a semantic problem when it comes to the church. We use the word *church* in so many ways that we often lose touch with the reality for which it stands. We use the word *church,* for example, to refer to the church building. We may say to a friend, "I will meet you at the church." It is not necessarily wrong to use the word in this way. When we do so, we make use of a form of shorthand with which we all are familiar. In a real, if limited, sense the church is a building. The building is where the church meets, and often the building plays a part in what the church does. The building in which one was married, the sanctuary in which one first felt the Spirit of God at work in one's life, the chapel from which one's parents were buried, may become very important places to people.

Places can become too important to people. Sometimes places become more important to people than people. Many churches are beset by an idolatry of place. Nevertheless, buildings are important to the church, not only because they provide sanctuaries of meaning but because they are concrete reminders to all who pass by that the church of Jesus Christ really and truly exists. They often symbolize the quality and character of a people's faith. The manner in which a church building and its grounds are maintained, how Christian people treat that part of God's creation entrusted to them, may speak volumes to the larger community concerning what those people really believe about God. Likewise, church property committees may consist of many unsung heroes in a local congregation, whose commitment to evangelism and social witness is worked out through the loving care they give to the physical face of the church. And yet, the church is always more than a building. The Puritans were technically accurate when they called their church buildings "meetinghouses," for the building is where the church meets.

We also use the word *church* to refer to some particular activity of the Christian community. We say, "I went to church last Sunday," when we really mean worship or church school. Sometimes we use the word *church* to refer to the institution as a whole, as when we give our money to the church or do church work. Neither use of the word is wrong, but we do need to be clear about what we mean when we speak in this way. The activities of the church are crucial to its existence, health, and growth. Good organization and faithful volunteers are necessary if the church is to actualize itself in programs and effective institutional forms. But activities and institutions are not the church. They are the ways and means of church life in the world of calendars, schedules, and organizational structures.

All too often the word *church* is defined by social and cultural characteristics, so that when people think of church they think of those particular things. There is a story attributed to the late George MacLeod, whose name is closely associated with the Iona community in Scotland, about a little Scottish city in which there were five churches, each located in just the right place in terms of its social and cultural characteristics. The Baptist church was near the river, the Salvation Army was by the firehouse, the Methodist church was next to the gas station, the Episcopal church was by the drapery store, and the Presbyterian church was halfway between the ice house and the bank. Stories like that are both humorous and tragic, indicating how easily the reality of the church of Jesus Christ is distorted by the cultural characteristics of its membership. How does one distinguish the true church from the buildings, activities, institutions, and cultural peculiarities of its members? If the church is the people of God, how does one recognize its existence in the churches?

THE CHURCH AND THE CHURCHES

The same question was raised in the early Christian community. At times we may be tempted to look back on the early Christian koinonia in an overly romantic and sentimental way, as if the early church had no problems with which to contend. In truth, they were as human and as fallible as we, forgiven sinners yet sinners still, in dire need of God's grace. Paul's Corinthian letters, for instance, evidence his great displeasure with the existing state of the church in Corinth. It was riddled with problems, not the least of which were quarreling, boasting, jealousy, strife, incest, lust, idolatry, gluttony, and drunkenness! Anyone of that time who looked very closely at the membership of the church in Corinth, or in any other town for that matter, could see that the actual fell far short of the ideal. There were members of the church then, as there are now, who simply were not viable candidates for heaven. Hypocrites and authentic believers were so intermingled in the Christian community that one could scarcely tell them apart. Soon it became all too clear that the true church of God, in and through which

God would renovate the fallen world, could not be unequivocally identified with the membership rolls of the churches. This incongruity between the ideal and the actual forced the Christian community to face the question: How is the true church of God to be distinguished from the pretender? How can one tell if a particular group of people that uses the word "church" is the true church of God?

The question was as difficult to answer then as it is now. Christians were not of one mind by any means about what makes the church the church. Some said that the existence of the true church depends on the existence of the sacraments, the means of grace. Irenaeus, a second-century theologian, said, "Where the Church is, there is the Spirit of God; and where the Spirit of God is, there is the Church, and every kind of grace," but apparently he attached the Spirit's presence to the existence of the sacrament of Baptism or the Lord's Supper, or both.[2] Others claimed that where the bishop was, there was the church. They felt that the church itself was the primary means of grace, since it was the context in which the sacraments were administered and received. Thus, the existence of the church depended upon the existence of the episcopate, the bishops ordained in apostolic succession for the ministry of the altar. "Therefore you must know that the bishop is in the church and the church is in the bishop," said Cyprian in the third century, "and that if somebody is not with the bishop, he is not in the church."[3] This view of the church, which Paul Tillich called "the purest form of episcopalianism," prevailed until the time of the Protestant Reformation.

THE MARKS OF THE CHURCH

One way to approach the question of how the true church is to be distinguished from the false is to consider the ancient marks or notes of the church. Ever since the Council of Constantinople in A.D. 381, Christians have confessed that the true church of God is one, holy, catholic, and apostolic. These four adjectives, arrived at by conflating the assertions made concerning the church in the Apostles' and Nicene Creeds, represent the marks or notes by which the true church is to be recognized. Most Christians, be they Roman Catholic, Orthodox, or Protestant, would agree that the true church is one, holy, catholic, and apostolic. But not all Christians would agree on what those four marks of the church mean.

The Reformers affirmed the four marks of the church along with the medieval church, but they did not agree with the medieval theologians on how they were to be interpreted. The Reformers stressed their adherence to the ancient creeds of the church, which defined the true church as one, holy, catholic, and apostolic, but they felt that the unity, holiness, catholicity, and apostolicity of the church existed only where the gospel was preached and heard and the sacraments administered according to their original intent. We can understand why they believed this. In the medieval church, the gospel in preaching, in the sacraments, and in the life of the Christian was often obscured by the abuses and distortions of traditions that had gained currency over the centuries. The Reformers felt that the unity, holiness, catholicity, and apostolicity of the medieval church were endangered because they were not rooted and grounded in prophetic preaching, faithful hearing, and the proper administration of the sacraments. They felt that the meaning of these four marks of the church, found in the New Testament, had essentially been lost. Thus, while the Reformers continued to affirm the four marks of the church, they gave to them a particular nuance or twist that clarified them in a new way.

The Reformers sought to clarify the ancient marks of the church, first, by defining the church in terms of the divine activity, asserting that the church is the people of God, created by God's Word and Spirit. Some of them resisted the notion that the church is defined by virtue of the fact that it is the seat and source of the sacraments, or that the church is dependent for its essential being on a system of priests ordained in apostolic succession. The church belongs to God. God created the church and apart from God the church would not be. Furthermore, God established Jesus Christ as the head and called the church to be his body, God's instrument for the renovation of the world. The identity of the church is to be found in God's call or election and in the church's servanthood after the example of Christ. Reformed Christians, therefore, tied the existence of the church to the existence of Jesus Christ. They agreed with Ignatius, who said in the second century, "Where Christ is, there is the Church." The true church exists wherever Jesus Christ is present in the world, wherever God calls people to be his body, and wherever men and women respond in faith and obedience.

In the second place, the Reformers sought to clarify the ancient marks of the church by perpetuating and restating the distinction that had long been made between the invisible and the visible church. How is one to reckon with the fact that the true church is so hard to find? The distinction between the invisible and the visible church was an attempt to say that the existence of the true church as a historical reality is known only to God and thus is apprehended by us only by faith.

This distinction between the invisible and the visible church was clearly formulated by Augustine in the fourth century. Augustine was steeped in Neoplatonic ways of thought. Platonists believed that true reality is not what is visible. True reality is invisible. The visible reality may well reflect the invisible, but when it does, it always reflects it in a partial and an imperfect way. Augustine viewed the world as a world in the process of becoming, the visible forms of which are real but imperfect reflections of the intelligible world of ideal forms. He understood the world as involved in tension and change, always on the way to a more perfect expression of the ideal in the actual. This worldview greatly influenced Augustine's doctrine of the church and that of the Reformers centuries later. The true church, according to Augustine, is always invisible. The visible church on earth is a real but imperfect reflection or representation of the true and invisible church, which is completely known only to God. We see the visible church, but we must believe that the invisible church exists in, but also above and beyond, its earthly form.

In the Middle Ages, the idea of the invisible church in which the visible participates but that can never be captured or exhausted by visible forms continued to exercise great influence on the church's self-understanding. Each celebration of the mass brought the invisible church to mind. There exists an invisible communion of saints, of which the believer was reminded at the Eucharist, whose membership is known only to God. In some aspects of the church's life, however, such as the practices surrounding the idea of vicarious merit and the primacy of the bishop of Rome, the idea of the invisible church lost much of its human character. It was radical thinkers, like John Wyclif and John Hus, who recaptured the twofold nature of the church as invisible and visible, which had grown out of Augustine's Neoplatonism. Wyclif argued in the fourteenth century that the true church is made up of those elected by God and is invisible to the human eye, an argument that threatened the very foundation of the medieval system. Hus, a bit later, tried to make a distinction between the holy catholic church and the Roman Catholic Church. The holy catholic church, he said, consists of the whole body of the predestinate, the living, the dead, as well as those yet unborn, and is known only to God. Peter may have been the head of the Roman Catholic Church, but he was never the head of the holy catholic church. Both men were Augustinians, Reformers before the Reformation, who sought to distinguish the true church of God from its imperfect historical form, and they passed that task on to the Protestant Reformers of later years.

Martin Luther read John Hus's treatise on the church, "De Ecclesia," in 1519. In 1520, Luther wrote to a friend that he was a Hussite without even knowing it and that he believed that Paul was as well![4] Luther was greatly influenced by Augustine's doctrine of the church, although Luther stressed its human, social, and ethical implications rather than the theoretical, metaphysical implications emphasized by Augustine. Luther cared more about how the invisible church manifested itself in the visible, historical, and communal structures of the world, while Augustine was more concerned to ground the imperfect church of this world in the invisible communion known only to God. For Luther, the true church is the mystical body of Christ, not the visible organization, but the invisible church is always present in the visible. The true church of God consists of all men and women of every time and place who laid hold on salvation by the faith implanted in them by God's Word and Spirit. The sacrament of the Lord's Supper, for Martin Luther, is the clearest manifestation and celebration of what the true church really is: the communion of Christian people with Christ and with one another, wholly visible only to God, but brought to visibility by the power of the Holy Spirit at work in the church on earth.

This view of the church was essentially shared by all of the Protestant Reformers. Luther and Calvin used different language to describe how people are included in the church. Luther spoke in terms of a human response to the faith implanted in the heart by God's Word and Spirit. Calvin spoke in terms of God's secret election since before the world began. But both essentially agreed on the nature of the church. Calvin noted that the word *church* is used in two ways in the Bible.[5] On the one hand, the Bible defines the church as "that which is actually in God's presence . . . not only the saints presently living on earth, but all the elect from the beginning of the world."[6] On the other hand, the Bible uses the word *church* to refer to all men and women on earth who worship and serve God, a definition that includes the hypocrite as well as the true believer. What does one do when the invisible church, the true church of God, is hard to find? Calvin said in effect that the existence of the true church is a matter of faith. The best that one can do at times is to trust that the invisible church exists and to revere and keep communion with the visible, leaving the final judgment as to where one stops and the other starts up to God.

For the Protestant Reformers, the existence of the invisible church was both a source of encouragement and the seed of reforming ferment. Calvin, even in his darkest moments, never really doubted that the true church of God exists in the world, albeit at times in hiding places: "Therefore, though the melancholy desolation which surrounds us, seems to proclaim that there is nothing left of the Church, let us remember that the death of Christ is fruitful, and that God wonderfully preserves his Church as it were in hiding-places."[7] That faith has the power to encourage and sustain a person in times when personal tragedy or social chaos seem to have overcome the witness of the church. But the idea of the invisible church acted not only to comfort but also to challenge the church so to reform itself that the invisible church might be more visible in the world. The invisible or true church was the ferment in the visible institution that periodically broke through to reform and renew its life.

For contemporary Christians, perhaps, this "conviction of things not seen" may be more clearly expressed by one of our own time. E. B. White, writing in 1938 of the apparent demise of religion in America, discerns God's presence in the world, God's clear witness to himself, even when it appears in the negative. White writes with seriousness, but not without tongue in cheek:

> But the Lord is persistent and lingers in strange places. He enjoys an honorable position among typographers, for He is always upper case. He enjoys an unique legal status, too, in the "Act of God" code, where elemental violence affords exemption from responsibility. Germany thinks she is ousting the Lord, but she fools herself. I am sure that even in Germany holy words are still used in cussing; and though religion may be in abeyance in home or church, one can always find ample assurance in the God-damning of a nation, that one's Redeemer liveth.[8]

When we confess our faith in the church, we are saying that we believe that in this mixed body (*corpus mixtum*) of which Augustine spoke, the true church of God exists, even though sometimes we cannot see it or find it. Christ lives, albeit in unexpected and obscured places, as in a lowly cowshed, or on a dusty Galilean road, or on a hideous cross. Wherever Christ lives, Reformed Christians believe, there the church lives as well.

Once this Reformed nuance (the church as the people of God, and the church as invisible and visible) has been established, the ancient marks of the church (one, holy, catholic, and apostolic) fall into place as valid criteria of the true church of God. To say that the church is *one* is to confess that Christ is not divided, that unity is of the essence of the church, and that the visible church, with its schisms and divisions, is a church under judgment. Few things were said more strongly by the Protestant Reformers, by whom division actually came to the church, than that the church is one. God is one; Christ is one; the Holy Spirit is one; therefore, the church is one. This faith in the essential unity of the church has its basis in Scripture: "There is one body and one Spirit, just as you were called to the one hope of your calling, one Lord, one faith, one baptism, one God and Father of all, who is above all and through all and in all" (Eph. 4:4–6).

Wherever there is plurality in the church, it is always plurality within one church, for the one church of God is the only church there is. The unity of the true church is the mystery; the visible church divided is the form. The mystery is hidden in the form, and the form lives wholly by the mystery. Likewise, the church militant and the church triumphant are not two churches but one. The dead no less than the living share in the communion of saints. The living are drawn toward that completion of life in God already known by the dead, and the dead continue in "mystic sweet communion" with those who are yet alive. Furthermore, the story of the church in the Old Testament and the story of the church after Christ are not two stories but one. Both Testaments tell the one story of the people of God in and through whom God intends to renovate the fallen world.

If the church is one, we can speak of the several churches only as parts of the whole. Environment, language, and customs differ from time to time and from place to place. Unity does not imply uniformity. But the church that meets here to do this or that cannot be a different church from the one that meets there to do another thing. Each in its own place is the one church in that particular space and time. "The one Church exists in its totality in each of the individual communities."[9] Reformed Christians believe that the church is one in spite of what people do to it. Indeed, this is the theological basis for a representative church government and for all ecumenical concern. We are one in Jesus Christ, even though we do not often live and act like that. The mission of the church, therefore, is to be what it is, that its unity might be more visible in the world.

The Belhar Confession, adopted by the Synod of the Dutch Reformed Mission Church in session at Belhar, Cape Town, Republic of South Africa, in 1982, followed the declaration of a *status confessionis* in connection with the rejection of the defense of apartheid on moral and theological grounds. It begins,

> We believe that unity is . . . both a gift and an obligation for the Church of Jesus Christ; that through the working of God's Spirit it is a binding force, yet simultaneously a reality which must be earnestly pursued and sought: one which the people of God must continually be built up to attain; that this unity must become visible so that the world may believe; that separation, enmity, and hatred between people and groups is sin which Christ has already conquered, and accordingly that anything which threatens this unity may have no place in the Church and must be resisted.

The church, in the second place, is *holy*. We have discussed the word holy previously in our discussion of the communion of saints. We have said that the church is holy, not because its individual members are morally perfect but because God is holy and because the church is set apart by God for a particular ministry in and to the world. Both points may be illustrated by a reference to a particular incident in the fourth century in which the nature of the church was at stake. This incident is sometimes referred to as the Donatist controversy.

The Donatist controversy raised the question, "What is the connection between grace and perfection, or between the unity and the holiness of the church?"[10] In Africa in the fourth century, there was a double image of the church. The prevailing view of the church in Africa at that time depended on the ability to perceive the church as a group of people who were manifestly different from other people, representing an alternative to the unclean and perverse environment in which the church lived. What God was doing to renovate the fallen world, according to this point of view, was to create an obviously different community, a holy community composed of holy people, as an alternative to the fallen world. The controversy was occasioned by the fact that the moral landmarks that might be expected to mark a holy people were being erased by the rapid growth of the church. As the church grew, all kinds of people were being admitted to membership, not only those who were holy in their everyday lives. Anyone who desired to join the church was welcomed with open arms, and many people feared that the distinctiveness of the church as an alternative to the sinful world would soon be lost.

The Donatist controversy represented a disagreement over the nature of the church. The Donatist party within the church, named after one Donatus, a bishop who tried to uphold the purity of the church by expelling from its leadership all clergy who were apostate or immoral, claimed that the unity of the church depended upon its prior holiness. The Donatists demanded that the church be purged of those among its leadership who had betrayed the church under persecution or otherwise had manifested an unholy walk of life. Only that church was the true church of God in which the communion of saints was a communion of perfect saints. And, of course, only the Donatist party met these qualifications!

Augustine, often called the Doctor of Grace, rejected the Donatist position and led the fight against its becoming normative in the church. He had more confidence in the power of God and in the resiliency of the church than the Donatists. Augustine believed that the church of God could absorb the world without losing its essential identity. It was his conviction that the essential identity of the church, its holiness, depended not on the purity of its leadership but on the identity or the holiness of God. Augustine was not nearly as interested in maintaining the perfection of the church as he was in furthering the mission of the church. He was concerned that the church of Christ be built and established throughout the world, and he felt that the time for this had come. Augustine's attitude toward the Donatists was one of contempt mixed with humor. At least once, he called the Donatists frogs and pictured them sitting in a marsh, croaking about their own salvation, while the world waited for the building of Christ's church: "The clouds of heaven thunder out throughout the world that God's house is being built; and the frogs cry from the marsh, We alone are Christians."[11]

Augustine conceived of the church as a healing community, the imperfect yet true manifestation of God's renovating activity in the world. He took no comfort in the sinfulness of the church or in the weakness of believers under fire, nor did he advocate "that ecclesiastical discipline should be set at naught, and that everyone should be allowed to do exactly as he pleased without any check, without a kind of healing chastisement, a lenity which should inspire fear, the severity of love."[12] Augustine simply believed that behavioral matters should be left to the polity of the church and not be the subject of doctrine. Those who misbehave or fail to make an adequate witness to Christ in times of persecution should be dealt with contextually according to existing rules of discipline, but they in no sense repudiate the essential holiness of the church. The holiness of the church is not dependent upon the moral perfection of the membership but on the holiness of God. The church is holy, and members of the church are called "saints," because the holy God has called the church and set people apart to be his own.

Third, the church is *catholic*. Reformed theologians have never been willing to give away the word *catholic* to the Roman See. *Catholic* means "general, comprehensive, whole, universal." To affirm that the church is catholic is to affirm the reality of a universal, comprehensive Christian church in which people of both sexes, and all races, classes, nations, kinds, and types who confess Jesus as Lord are included. The catholic church is the inclusive church. Cyril of Jerusalem wrote in his catechetical lectures in A.D. 350 the following description of the catholic church:

> The Church, then, is called Catholic because it is spread through the whole world, from one end of the earth to the other, and because it never stops teaching in all its fullness every doctrine that men ought to be brought to know: and that regarding things visible and invisible, in heaven and on earth.[13]

The church is also called catholic because it consists of a pluralism of need, and cherishes a pluralism of race, class, social standing, and individual ability, in its membership. Cyril goes on to say:

> It is called Catholic because it brings into religious obedience every sort of men, rulers and ruled, learned and simple, and because it is a universal treatment and cure for every kind of sin whether perpetrated by soul or body, and possesses within it every form of virtue that is named, whether it expresses itself in deeds or words or in spiritual graces of every description.[14]

The catholicity of the church is always threatened by the natural human instinct for homogeneous associations and relationships. Inner-city churches may represent a measure of pluralism due to the social composition of the neighborhood in which they are set, but the suburban congregation, located in a neigh-borhood that is segregated by race, class, or economic condition, often has trouble manifesting the catholicity of the church. Furthermore, the Reformed faith has always had a special appeal to middle-class people; consequently, Reformed churches have often been middle-class churches. In one sense, this fact offers these churches great opportunities to shape the culture of which they are a part, since their pews are filled on Sunday mornings with the business and professional people who regularly influence the decisions and directions of the society at large. In another sense, however, the homogeneity of the typical Reformed congregation has obscured one of the essential marks of the church, namely, its catholicity. Human differences are gifts of God to the church, and each congregation must strive to be inclusive of all sorts and conditions of people if it is to manifest true catholicity in its fellowship. There is no one way of being Christian. The catholicity of the church means that the church can and should tolerate various ways of being Christian within its fellowship.

The Reformed doctrine of the church assumes that no local congregation of Christian people can be the church if it does not manifest the catholicity of the church. Presbyterians seek to manifest the catholicity of the church through church courts or judicatories composed of ministers of the Word and ruling elders. In their participation in these governing bodies, ministers and elders who have been elected by the people share the common life of the church catholic and seek God's will concerning its worship and work. We shall say more about Presbyterian polity in a later chapter. Suffice it to say here that the system of representative government is the attempt of the Reformed community to participate in the whole body of believers. Through these church courts, Reformed people are related to the life of the denomination and, through interdenominational organizations such as the National and World Councils of Churches, to the church throughout the nation and world.

The statement of the Commission on Faith and Order of the World Council of Churches in 1982 is a remarkable attempt to witness to the essential catholicity of the church. Representatives of virtually all confessional traditions, including the Roman Catholic, participated in a process of discussion and clarification that resulted in a harmonious statement concerning such crucial areas as baptism, the Eucharist, and ministry. The statement calls for mutual recognition of baptism "as an important sign and means of expressing the baptismal unity given in Christ."[15] It seeks to underscore points of agreement in the theory and practice of the various communions in regard to the Lord's Supper, in the conviction that "the increased mutual understanding expressed in the present statement may allow some churches to attain a greater measure of eucharistic communion among themselves and so bring closer the day when Christ's divided people will be visibly reunited around the Lord's Table."[16]

The document also calls for a mutual recognition of the ordained ministries, with special attention given to the issue of apostolic succession. Churches that have preserved apostolic succession are asked to recognize the apostolic content of the ordained ministry in churches that have not maintained such succession. Churches without episcopal succession, but living in faithful continuity with the apostolic tradition, are asked to realize that the continuity of the apostolic church finds profound expression in the successive laying on of hands by bishops, and suggests that this sign serves to strengthen and deepen that continuity.[17] This statement is binding on no denomination and is offered for study by all, but it is a document unprecedented in the ecumenical movement in its attempt to manifest the essential catholicity of the church.

In the fourth place, the true church of God is *apostolic*. The word *apostolic* is not often used by Reformed people, but the faith that the church is apostolic lies at the very heart of the Reformed doctrine of the church. Apostolic means "in the discipleship, in the school, under the normative authority, instruction and direction of the apostles, in agreement with them, because listening to them and accepting their message."[18] Some Christians hold that the apostolicity of the church is grounded in the apostolic succession of its bishops. Reformed theologians have felt that apostolicity cannot be based on historical or juridical grounds. To do so would be to understand the apostolicity of the church in mechanical ways, obviating both the work of the Holy Spirit and the faith of the believing community. In that case, Karl Barth suggested, all we would need is archaeological knowledge of the list of bishops in order to determine where the true church exists.[19] When Reformed people confess that the church is apostolic, however, they affirm their continuity with the apostolic testimony and mission. Apostolicity, like the other marks of the church, is a gift of God and must be received by faith. It can never be achieved or protected by institutional processes. Apostolicity is evidence of the Spirit's activity in the life and work of the church from one generation to another.

The apostles were people of great importance in the early church. The first Christians depended heavily on the firsthand witness of the apostles and granted to them great authority in matters of faith and practice. As time went by, the witness of the apostles was kept alive by teaching, preaching, and by correspondence between congregations. The mission of the apostles, summarized in the great commission to witness to Christ to the ends of the earth, became the mission of the whole church. The apostolic testimony and mission come to us through the Bible. Thus, the apostolic church today will be the church that lives close to the Bible. To say that the church is apostolic is to affirm the fact that the true church is the church that lives in continuity with the apostles, that confesses the apostolic faith, and that accepts the apostolic mission as its own.

In summary, the Protestant Reformers tried to say what the ancient marks of the church really mean. The very existence of reform movements that resulted in division called into question the identity and location of the church. Which church was to be considered the true church? The medieval church also held that the church is one, holy, catholic, and apostolic. The Reformers sought to clarify these ancient marks of the church in terms of the gospel of Jesus Christ. They affirmed that the true church may be discerned wherever the Word is rightly preached and the sacraments rightly administered. At times, Calvin added discipline to these marks of the church, but discipline was clearly subordinate to the other two marks. Calvin said, "Wherever we see the Word of God purely preached and heard, and the sacraments administered according to Christ's institution, there, it is not to be doubted, a church of God exists.[20]

Most Reformed confessions (e.g., the Augsburg Confession, the Geneva Catechism, the Scots Confession, the Belgic Confession, the Heidelberg Catechism) said essentially the same thing, making the point that the existence of the church depends on Christ and none other, and on the response to him in faith. Wherever Christ is present in Word and sacrament, wherever people respond in faith and obedience, there the church exists as the body of Christ. There Christ gives to the church its unity, holiness, catholicity, and apostolicity.

Karl Barth issued a corrective word of warning concerning the contemporary relevance of these marks of the church.[21] He commented that there is a "yawning gap" in the Reformed doctrine of the church, created by the absence of any sense of the church's mission in and to the world. Barth put fundamental questions to Reformed ecclesiology. Why does the church exist? Where does the church exist? Why the Word and the sacraments? Why Christ? What is the meaning and purpose of the church that exists in Christ on the basis of the preaching of the Word and the celebration of the sacraments? Is the church an end in itself? Surely God did not create the church only to be the mother of the faithful. Barth calls this the holy egoism of the church. The truth of the matter is that the church exists for the world. It is the community of believers that God has sent out into the world to proclaim the good news of what God has done and is doing to restore the fallen creation. The church "is the point in the world where its eyes are opened to itself and an end is put to its ignorance about itself."[22] The church exists, then, not only where the Word is preached and the sacraments are celebrated but wherever the will and work of God is proclaimed and done in the world. Mission is the third mark of the church.

IS THERE SALVATION
OUTSIDE THE CHURCH?

The true church of God has occupied much of our attention thus far. We have asked after its necessity, defined it in terms of the communion of saints and the priesthood of all believers, and distinguished it from all other groups of people by means of its unity, holiness, catholicity, and apostolicity. One question lingers to haunt us: Granted that the church is necessary, how necessary is it? Is there salvation outside the church? Many people throughout the history of the church, with varying interpretations, have maintained that *extra ecclesiam nulla salus,* outside the church there is no salvation. Both Luther and Calvin took that position. The Westminster Confession of Faith specifically declares that there is no ordinary possibility of salvation outside the church (6.126). Most of us today consider ourselves too sophisticated or liberal of heart for such a hard stricture. However that may be, before we dismiss the matter out of hand, we do well to ask what was originally meant by this statement. Perhaps we will find that our discomfort with the idea stems not from our sophistication or our liberality but from our lack of familiarity with the experience of salvation of which the statement speaks.

The claim that outside the church there is no salvation may be best understood in its original intent as a negative formulation of a positive conviction. It may well have originated early on in the Christian community, not as a doctrine but as the experience of believers. Men and women living in those first centuries after Christ actually did find salvation—meaning, purpose, hope, forgiveness, health, wholeness—inside and not outside the church. Life outside the church was driven by power and pleasure and blessed by a pantheon of gods of the culture's own making. Life inside the church was different, so radically different, in fact, that the boundary line between the two became clear and distinct. When Christians claimed that outside the church there is no salvation, they were stating a matter of fact that they daily and personally experienced. The presence and power of God in Christ to change life and to inform life with meaning and purpose was so real that life outside the church seemed shallow indeed.

Later, as the church reflected on the experience of those first Christians and tried to make some systematic sense of it all, the claim that outside the church there is no salvation took a different turn. Instead of an expression of Christian joy in the quality of life experienced in the Christian koinonia, *extra ecclesiam nulla salus* became a harsh and restrictive means of institutional identity and power. The doctrinal formulation was stated most clearly by Cyprian in the third century as a means of affirming the essential unity of the church. He believed that the one, holy, catholic, and apostolic church was not simply a community of Christian people, a society of believers, or even the sum of all its parts, but the sole ark of salvation outside of which no one could be saved. After all, the church was the one visible body that cherished the apostolic writings, including the Scriptures of ancient Israel, treasured the apostolic tradition, and organized itself under a succession of bishops through which these things had been handed down. Cyprian believed that Christians may or may not be united inwardly and spiritually but that the unity of the church is a fact, that the church's unity cannot be broken. Outside that unity there is no church, according to Cyprian, and thus no salvation. The Holy Spirit and the means of grace were bestowed by Christ upon the church alone, and apart from the church no one is saved.

Today the boundary line between the church and the world is not nearly as clear as it once was. Why is that so? Has the church so completely penetrated the world with its own spirit that the world is more Christian today than it was when people said *extra ecclesiam nulla salus?* Many institutions and values of contemporary society do reflect the influence of the Christian church, but only the romantics among us would claim that we live in a Christian world wherein church and world are essentially one. The more likely reason for the indistinct boundary between church and world is that the world has so infiltrated the church that salvation—this release from sin and guilt, reconciliation with God and neighbor, the peace and joy in a quality of life where love norms even faith and hope, and the forward-look of the resurrection of the partial and incomplete when all things broken will be mended and all things dead given new life, so keenly experienced by those early Christians—is essentially foreign to people today.

Furthermore, although Cyprian's teaching was clear and coherent, holding the church together in an intelligible and salutary way, it had terrible theological and pastoral consequences. The promise of salvation was withheld from millions of people, even people of faith, because they were outside the institutional church. Profound questions have been raised against this doctrine. Cannot, does not, the Holy Spirit operate outside the church? Is God so parochial? Cannot, does not, God save whomever God pleases to save, regardless of institutional identification? Is the church the kingdom of God exclusively, and if so, which church? Are the means of grace, particularly the sacraments of Baptism and the Lord's Supper, necessary for salvation? The Reformers knew that the church is necessary if the believer is to be strengthened and nurtured, but they also knew that salvation is by grace through faith. Thus, they could not finally say *extra ecclesiam nulla salus.* The Second Helvetic Confession comes close, but its emphasis is placed not on the institution but on the fellowship to which Christ offers himself to be enjoyed. The confession states that there is "no certain salvation" outside of Christ, who gives himself to the church, that those who wish to live in him "must in no wise separate themselves from the true Church of Christ."[23]

However, before we dismiss the idea of *extra ecclesiam nulla salus* altogether, we do well to recall that the church is a part of the gospel, one of the ways that God has identified with our finitude and weakness. The church is the ordinary context of God's justifying and sanctifying activity, where people hear the gospel, respond in faith, grow in grace, live in hope, and are equipped for service in the world. If this is what we mean by salvation, then it is not at all clear that it is found outside the church except in extraordinary circumstances. If the church, even in a partial and provisional way, is God's renovating activity in the world, then there is a sense in which Christians are included in what God is doing in and through their membership in the church.

The problem with this assertion is that it would surely be misunderstood if so stated today. Christians must be careful with any assertion that might appear to limit the power and activity of God to include whomever God wills to include in God's renovating activity in the world. We must be careful, first, because of what we know about historical relativism. That which our forebears considered necessary for salvation may not be considered so by us. Many convictions are changed, expanded, altered, or jettisoned altogether in the light of new knowledge or illuminating historical circumstances. No one generation can set the conditions of salvation for another without assuming too much for itself.

Second, we must be careful because of what we learn from other religions. We are slowly learning that world missions, for example, is not simply a matter of bringing God to the pagans or converting the heathen to the truth. We have learned that many people outside the church have something important to say to people inside the church about who God is, how God is known and experienced, and what God expects of us.

Third, we must be careful because of what we know about the ambiguity of the church itself, the development of its doctrine, and the formation of its dogma. The question the church must put to itself before it looks at others is whether there is salvation inside the church! The imperfections, or better, the sinfulness of the church precludes any easy judgment to the effect that those outside are unsaved. When parables of the kingdom, reflections of the truth, and genuine virtue appear outside the church, we should accept them gratefully as testimony to the sovereignty of God and the lordship of Christ. Jesus said, "I have other sheep that do not belong to this fold" (John 10:16), a word that the church forgets at its own expense.

Therefore, although we may yet believe that the claim, outside the church there is no salvation, once may have told the truth and may yet remind us of certain things long forgotten, Christians are well advised to beware of its use today. There are other ways to suggest that salvation draws people into the community of faith. The task of the church is to be the church and to leave ultimate judgments concerning the fate of other people to God. It is to demonstrate to people outside the church that there is salvation to be found within the church, regardless of where else it may or may not be found, and to invite them to share its benefits.

Chapter 6

The Humanity
of the Church

*We are reproached because there have been manifold dissensions
and strife in our churches since they separated themselves from the
Church of Rome, and therefore cannot be true churches. . . .
[T]here have at all times been great contentions in the Church,
and the most excellent teachers of the Church have differed among
themselves about important matters without meanwhile the
Church ceasing to be the Church because of these contentions. For
thus it pleases God to use the dissensions that arise in the Church to
the glory of his name, to illustrate the truth, and in order that those
who are in the right might be manifest (1 Cor. 11:19).*
Second Helvetic Confession

Reformed ecclesiology is rooted and grounded in the conviction that the church
is an act of God, called into being by God's Word and sustained by God's Spirit,
the provisional demonstration and instrument of God's unparalleled renovation
of the fallen world. The church is the people of God, the communion of saints,
the priesthood of believers—one, holy, catholic, and apostolic—into which men
and women are called and nurtured by Word and sacrament. "But we have this
treasure in clay jars, so that it may be made clear that this extraordinary power
belongs to God and does not come from us" (2 Cor. 4:7).

That is to say, if we are to understand the Reformed doctrine of the church
aright, we must view it from below as well as from above. We must understand
it as a human, historical, limited institution that functions like any other institution in society. In this chapter, therefore, we will look at the humanity of the
church in an effort to discern the nature of the earthen vessels and to assess their

importance to Christian faith and life, that we may not forget "that this extraordinary power belongs to God and does not come from us."

Earthen vessels are always imperfect, easily broken and constantly in need of repair. They never quite do justice to the splendor of the treasure they hold. Christians generally agree that the treasure is Jesus Christ, who is "the same yesterday and today and forever" (Heb. 13:8), but Christians have not always been of one mind as to the nature of the vessel. Sometimes Christians have equated the treasure with the vessel, forgetting that the vessel is of this earth and thus imperfect. At other times, Christians have assumed that they could have the treasure independent of the vessel, making the vessel essentially unnecessary. Neither position adequately maintains the tension between the ideal and the actual, between the church as we believe it to be and that which we experience in our historical lives. Reformed Christians maintain that apart from the treasure the church is nothing. But we also know that, apart from the realization that the vessel is of this earth, the treasure itself is perverted.

We have said that the Protestant Reformers perpetuated the Augustinian distinction between the invisible and the visible church. This distinction makes a positive contribution to our understanding of the existence of the true church as a matter of faith. We believe that the true church of God exists even though we do not always see it take shape in our churches. The negative side of that distinction, however, is that it provides a person with a convenient escape hatch through which to exit when the going gets tough in the visible church. It gives one a way out when the church shows itself to be disappointing, unfaithful, unimaginative, self-serving, and weak. It enables one to relinquish responsibility for the church and to withdraw from its membership when the actual does not live up to the ideal.

To affirm the humanity of the church as an integral part of the true church, to suggest that the fumbling institution located at the corner of X and Y streets is a part of the ontology (being or essence) of the true church, is to affirm that God uses ordinary human, historical realities to accomplish the divine purposes on and for the earth. The church is always more than meets the eye, but it includes that which meets the eye. It has a visible structure for which no apology need be made. Reformed Christians freely admit that there is great diversity in the visible church. There are many legitimate ways of being Christian, various historical families or traditions of faith and life, and many ways of being faithful to the particular tradition of which one is a part. The conviction that the church exists wherever the Word is rightly preached and the sacraments rightly administered, coupled with the willingness to leave the word *rightly* to the church to define, makes the Reformed doctrine of the church one of the most inclusive to be found anywhere. Since there is such latitude within the Reformed tradition and within the Reformed doctrine of the church, and since churches of every tradition share the basic humanity of which we speak, we shall deal with the human nature of the church in general, suggesting as we go the particular nuances that make a particular church Reformed.

WHAT IS THE HUMANITY
OF THE CHURCH?

How does one define the humanity of the church? When seen from below, the church may be viewed as a visible human community, "an historically continuous body of persons known as Christians, whose common life is in part institutionalized in churches."[1] It is the activity of men and women in particular times and particular places who more or less share their lives in groups that are identifiable by certain operational habits, organizational methods, institutional forms, means of communication, and modes of thought and speech. It is a voluntary association of men and women who are bound together by a common loyalty, certain constitutive events, a commonly agreed upon collection of source materials, and a set of representative symbols. The church is a social movement comprised of people who more or less live a separate existence, yet together seek to influence the society at large. It is a political community, organized under a certain polity or form of government, within which people employ political skills and processes to make the structures of the community responsive to their understanding of its reason for being. In short, when viewed from below, the church is not unfamiliar to us. It is a human community not unlike other human communities. It is an organization that functions very much like other organizations we know.

Claude Welch reminds us that the New Testament is well aware of the humanity of the church. The church as a believing, responding people is taken for granted in the New Testament. The word *ecclesia,* which literally means "those called out" or "the summoned people," is often used in the New Testament to refer to the church in its purely historical manifestation: the seven churches in Asia (Rev. 1:4), the "church throughout all Judea and Galilee" (Acts 9:31), "every church" (Acts 14:23), "all the churches of the Gentiles" (Rom. 16:4), "all the churches of Christ" (Rom. 16:16), the church laid waste (Acts 8:3), and the many references to the church as a community of Christian people. Welch notes that in instances such as these, the reference is to a group of human beings in some particular time and place. There is no theological or ecclesiological significance to these references. "On the contrary," Welch suggests, "these passages are important precisely because they express what is taken for granted throughout the New Testament, that the church is patently and indisputably (we might even say, first of all) a human community responding. This belongs to the essence, the ontology, of the church."[2] However exalted the New Testament view of the church, and implicit in its discussion of the church as the body of Christ, there is always the knowledge that the church is a concrete historical reality, a body of human beings in time and space, living in response to the activity of God.

When God acts, people respond. God's activity creates a responding people. The human response to God is used of God and becomes a part of God's continuing activity in the world. Thus, the author of Acts 2:42–47 describes the response of the early church to the proclamation of the gospel as an integral part of God's will and work. We are told that those first believers devoted themselves to various activities that were likely to strengthen their faith, deepen their worship, and quicken their sense of mission in the world. They concentrated their attention on apostolic teaching as they sought to understand as well as to experience what they believed. They engaged in various fellowship activities. They ate together, prayed together, worshiped together, and had all things in common. The author of Acts was well aware of the fact that the church is not the kingdom of God, just as we are aware of the fact that natural science is not nature. Just as natural science is the human response to the world of nature, so the church, which traces its origin to the divine initiative, is the human response to God, "the subjective pole of the objective rule of God."[3] The church is a human community, a responding people, a group of men and women in a particular time and place who seek to answer God's call with their lives.

The humanity of the church ought to be more than obvious to us, but is it? Our attitudes and actions sometimes betray a higher doctrine of the church than our theology should allow. In truth, most of us are tempted at one time or another to some form of ecclesiastical docetism. *Docetism,* which comes from a Greek word that means "to appear," usually refers to the belief that Jesus Christ was truly God but only appeared to be a man. Long ago the church declared that docetism is an inadequate view of the incarnation. Jesus Christ was truly God, but he was also a real man. Sometimes our churchly attitudes and actions are docetic in the sense that they fail to take adequate account of the true humanity of the church.

The Protestant Reformers felt that the humanity of the church had been lost in the medieval period and they sought to recover it. Yet many theologies of the church, even within contemporary Protestantism, still fail to do it justice. Emil Brunner, for example, the Swiss Reformed theologian, wrote in 1952, "The New Testament Ecclesia, the fellowship of Jesus Christ, is a pure communion of persons and has nothing of the character of an institution about it."[4] The humanity of the church is obscured when the church is defined as a pure communion with nothing of the character of an institution about it. The human nature of the church is lost whenever the church is uncritically equated with the kingdom of God.

Ecclesiastical docetism is not limited to the theologies or the theologians of the church. It crops up in many of our everyday attitudes and actions. We often expect too much from the church, for instance, as though it were somehow above and beyond error, then accuse it of hypocrisy when it proves to be all too human. We associate the church with the realm of the spiritual and are offended when it manifests its concern with material things, such as meeting a budget or providing low-cost housing for the poor. We set our ministers and lay leaders on a pedestal, forgetting that they are ordinary human beings, and are personally offended when they fail or fall.

Ministers themselves, as they attend to the endless details of church administration, are often tempted by a docetic view of the church. In situations of tragedy or grief, details such as the placement of the casket, the use of flowers, the need for extra janitorial help, and the provision for adequate parking appear embarrassingly trivial compared to the profound emotional and spiritual needs of the moment. The pathos of the human condition is so stark and poignant that the practical details of administering an institutional church seem unrelentingly this-worldly and crass in contrast. Doctors, lawyers, undertakers, food caterers, flower merchants, even friends on the block feel no need to apologize for attending to the practical details of ministering to the moment, whereas the minister, the sup-posed mediator of holy things, is under no little pressure to bring the material and the spiritual worlds together in ways that people with unsophisticated theo-logical backgrounds can comprehend. These feelings are natural and not all bad. They may reveal a minister's reverent awareness of the inevitable ambiguity of all historical situations in which the divine and the human intersect. They may issue in a ministry of compassion, humility, and sensitivity that will bear witness to the reality of that which he or she seeks to represent. But these feelings do hint at a docetic view of the church. If the church is truly human, we need not be ashamed of or embarrassed by the mundane details of its historical life. These very processes, including the seemingly endless round of details involved in church administration and pastoral care, are precisely the earthen vessels in and through which God has chosen to renovate the world.

In order better to understand the humanity of the church, we shall consider three of its more obvious institutional aspects: the church as a community of need, the church as a child of time and space, and the church as limited by temp-tation and sin.

THE HUMANITY OF THE CHURCH: A COMMUNITY OF NEED

When the church is viewed from below, it is seen as a community of human need. It is a congregation of men, women, and children—be it at a local, regional, national, or international level—who have basic physical, emotional, psycholog-ical, social, and spiritual needs. These needs include such things as food, shelter, acceptance, support, values, friendship, relationships, intimacy, stimulation, community, and meaning. When the church functions well as a human com-munity, it provides a connecting link between God's renovating activity in the world and the needs of people. This does not mean that the gospel of Jesus Christ is occasioned by the needs of people, nor does it compromise the divine initia-tive that the gospel proclaims. To the contrary, it affirms God's love and care for real people who have real needs. To view the church as a community of need is simply to admit that, unless the communication and celebration of the gospel are related to the needs of people, life in the Christian church becomes sterile, rou-tine, irrelevant, and very boring.

The Second Helvetic Confession, often called the most universal of all Reformed creeds, readily admits this fact. It was written in 1561 by Heinrich Bullinger of Zurich. Bullinger intended to attach it to his will as his legacy to the city of Zurich, but made it available instead to Frederick III of Germany, who in 1566 published the confession as the statement of his Reformed faith. Approximately one-half of this extensive Reformed creed is devoted to the church as a community of need, affirming and exploring the personal and practical occasions where the activity of God touches the needs of people. According to Edward A. Dowey, "The most remarkable achievement of the Confession is the way in which biblical and technical theological materials are expressed simply and always with a view to their practical significance for daily life."[5]

The significance of church life is acknowledged in the Second Helvetic Confession as in no other Reformed creed. For instance, it stresses the importance of humble, modest, public worship in the language of the people. It acknowledges that people can worship God at any time, but it knows that people are fickle and that certain times need to be planned and set apart for the worship of God.

> Although religion be not tied unto time, yet can it not be planted and exercised without a due dividing and allotting-out of time. Every Church, therefore, does choose unto itself a certain time for public prayers, and for the preaching of the Gospel, and for the celebration of the sacraments; and it is not lawful for any one to overthrow this appointment of the Church at his own pleasure. For except some due time and leisure were allotted to the outward exercise of religion, without doubt men would be quite drawn from it by their own affairs.[6]

The sacraments, though they are subordinated in importance to the preaching of the Word, are significant for the church because they are God's instruments "whereby he keeps in continual memory, and recalls to mind . . . his great benefits bestowed upon man."[7] The confession even takes dissension in the church seriously, suggesting that it may be used by God for the glory of God's name, to set forth truth and to clarify error.[8] Furthermore, the Second Helvetic Confession emphasizes the importance of teaching and of visiting the sick. In the attention given to the Christian education of youth, the ground is prepared for the church of the future.[9] In visiting the sick, the church relates the gospel to the most spiritually vulnerable time of all, the time of illness, assisting people in these times of physical weakness to resist temptation and doubt.[10] It concerns itself with the burial and care of the dead, with the place of ceremonies and rites, and with the importance of the care and use of property and possessions. Fully conscious of the fact that the church is an act of God, the confession nevertheless acknowledges without apology that the church is a community of need. It affirms the humanity of this responding people as an integral part of the Reformed doctrine of the church.

A good illustration of the church as a community of need is found in the importance of the kitchen in the church building. No one would think of building a church without a kitchen. Why are kitchens so important to the church? The answer is that kitchens provide the church with an instrument by means of which the gospel of Jesus Christ is related to a basic human need. Eating and drinking are two of the most basic human needs. People need to eat and drink in order to live. It is not without theological significance that Jesus came eating and drinking, that he often met people at mealtime, that he was moved with compassion when people were hungry and fed them, and that at least on one occasion "he was known to them in the breaking of the bread" (Luke 24:35). From the earliest days of the church, Christians gathered at table have sensed in their table fellowship the nearer presence of their Lord. Thus, a basic human need, the need for bodily nourishment, was transformed into a deeply religious occasion.

One cannot understand the significance of the sacrament of the Lord's Supper apart from the basic need for food and drink. Bread and wine have taken on a highly sophisticated theological significance in the life of the church at times, but they never lost touch with the need that first gave them their unique status as symbols. In the physical acts of eating and drinking, men and women partake of that which sustains and nurtures bodily life. In the physical acts of eating the bread and drinking the wine in the Lord's Supper, men and women partake of God's grace by faith for the sustenance and nurture of body and soul. The point is that the church is a community of need. Physical acts and activities occasioned by human need are occasions for profound religious experience. Kitchens, menus, bread, and wine, in God's hands, may become means of grace.

Another illustration of the church as a community of need is the manner in which the church tries to relate the faith it professes to the various times and seasons of life. The calendar, the dates and times of great significance in a person's life, may be occasions of grace. The times of birth, the passage from infancy to adulthood, marriage, death and dying are times for worship, teaching, and nurture. The church surrounds these times and seasons of life with ultimate meaning, human compassion, and significant relationships. In the case of childbirth, the church may give to the family of the newborn child a cradle cross, so that this symbol of the Christian faith might early become a part of the child's consciousness. In infant baptism, the church reaffirms its faith in a God who willed the child to be, a God for whom no human being is an accident, who gives to the child his or her unique identity and draws the child into the circle of God's covenant promises and love. In confirmation, the church celebrates a rite of passage in a person's life, marking the movement of a person from infancy toward maturity, granting the person the opportunity to confirm the vows taken on his or her behalf by parents at baptism, or certifying in believer's baptism that the person is now ready for adult participation in the life of the church.

Marriage is another important time of life that the church does not ignore. The Reformed tradition does not admit to marriage as a sacrament, but it does mark marriage as a time of worship and teaching. In premarital counseling, the church, through its minister or other designated representative, seeks to relate its insights and values to two people who intend to live together for the rest of their lives. In the marriage service, the man and the woman are charged to live together as heirs of the grace of life in the covenant of their God. Increasingly, the church is having to come to grips with broken marriages, with second or third marriages, and with new forms of human association, inside as well as outside its member-ship. Unwed parents who bear children, unwed parents who adopt children, single-parent families, and same-sex couples are often represented in the mem-bership of Christian churches today, and the church must find forms of worship, teaching, and nurture that are adequate for these new life situations. The church is not called upon to judge which person or which form of human association is acceptable in the sight of God, but it is called to witness to God's forgiveness and mercy in Jesus Christ to all sorts and conditions of people in relationships of love and commitment.

The time of death is a particularly important time in the life of the church. The fact of death raises ultimate questions both for those who sense its coming and to those who are left behind when a loved one dies. Physical death calls the assertion that life has meaning into radical question. It confronts the individual with the mystery into which and beyond which no one can see. Death as a fact of life often has the effect of drawing people closer together into a community of conversation, conviction, and compassion. The dying person usually wants to surround his or her dying with the language and symbols of faith and hope. Fam-ilies and friends are often open to any insights or convictions that bring a mea-sure of affirmation to bear upon their loss. When death occurs, the church gathers to thank God for the gift of life and for the life of the loved one departed, and offers its support through the liturgy by means of proclamation, hymns, Bible reading, and confession of faith. The funeral or memorial service is one of the most significant occasions in the life of the church, in the context of which the Christian faith is brought into contact with basic human need.

Since each new generation of Christians brings to light new and different needs, the church must always be prepared to develop new liturgical and pastoral forms with which to contextualize these needs. The church exists today in a soci-ety in which people are highly mobile, flexible, and open to change. A person may reassess career options in midlife and make an entirely new beginning. A family may reestablish its place of residence eight or ten times during its life together. A person may retire early in life and devote the remainder of his or her active days to public service. Children leave home for college or military service or employment in a distant city. Individuals or entire families may decide to undertake a new challenge, share a common task, or undertake a new venture involving uncommon sacrifice. Each new occasion in individual or family life offers the church the possibility of attaching its faith and values to the formative occasions of life.

Still other illustrations of the church as a community of need may be found in the many ways the church makes contact with the basic emotional, psychologi-cal, and social needs of people. The church, not unlike other social institutions, is an association of human beings with specific desires, dreams, and goals. This may appear to some to be a truism, though in truth it is not. The recent attempt to extend the impersonal approach of science and technology to organizations and institutions that, regardless of their size and reason for being, remain essentially human institutions, is evidence enough that the humanity of social institutions is often forgotten. According to J. Douglas Brown, "The initiating forces which control the behavior of an organization remain human and disparate even under the greatest pressures for cohesion and conformity. Human organizations persist in being human. Dictators have learned this to their sorrow."[11] A political party, a transnational corporation, a fraternity, a labor union, the hospital auxiliary, and a book club may have little in common except one very important thing, namely, the fact that, in their historical manifestation, they are all human institutions, composed of human beings, that offer to their constituencies certain emotional, psychological, and social rewards or benefits. Continued participation in the activities of these social organizations is directly related to their ability to relate the object of their concern to the needs and expectations of people.

The same is true for the church. Humanly speaking, participation in the life and work of a church is directly related to the church's ability to relate the gospel to the needs and expectations of its people. Sometimes the church does this most successfully in unprogrammed and spontaneous ways. When church members gather to paint a Sunday school room, the primary agenda is to paint the room, but significant things have been known to happen to people who paint rooms together in the context of the church. Without regard to wealth or status, two people, each with paintbrush in hand, may begin to know, trust, and even love each other in ways that affect the course of their lives. Barriers between them may fall; stereotypes may be shattered. When they finish painting the classroom, the basic human need for relationships that matter may have been met, not by having a program on how to relate to people but by bringing people together for a common task. The church is far from perfect and does not always succeed in relating the gospel to human needs, but there is no understanding of the scope of its task, or of the splendor of its opportunities, without understanding this as a part of it.

THE HUMANITY OF THE CHURCH:
A CHILD OF TIME AND SPACE

The church manifests its humanity in its existence as a community of human need. It also does so in its existence as a child of time and space. Jesus Christ is "the same yesterday and today and forever" (Heb. 13:8), but the church as a human community is born and lives in time and space. It is a historical community, and its forms of expression are relative to the particular time and place in which they gain currency. The church as a human institution consists of men and women who live, think, decide, and act in the context of a particular historical time and a certain geographical place. Their language, their categories of thought and communication, their understanding of God, like their politics, reflect the environment in which they live, as noted by H. Richard Niebuhr:

> The patterns and models we employ to understand the historical world may have had a heavenly origin, but as we know and use them they are, like ourselves, creatures of history and time; though we direct our thought to eternal and transcendent beings, it is not eternal and transcendent; though we regard the universal, the image of the universal in our mind is not a universal image.[12]

We are in time, but time is also in us, not only time in general but a particular time "of a definite society with distinct language, economic and political relations and social organization."[13] The church shares this historical relativism, as do all other forms of human association, and must respond to the eternal God as a child of time and space.

The fact of historical relativism does not necessarily deny the truth of that which the church confesses in various times and places. It does not mean that the faith of the church is merely the creature of a particular time and place, with little or no reference to that which is really true. It does keep before the church the fact that time-bound conceptualities, local customs, and parochial prejudices are often confused with the gospel. The history of Christian believing is full of false starts and wrong turns. Yet even in its darkest periods, when the church seemed most corrupt or in error, its faith and practice yet testified to the reality of God, to the person and work of Jesus Christ, and to the contemporary presence and power of the Holy Spirit, which gave to church doctrine and practice an amazing potential for rectification and reform. From the very beginning, the church has contained diverse traditions of faith and practice. The fact of historical relativism not only reminds us that all traditions are partial; it also reminds us that all traditions are subordinate to the one normative tradition, which is the revelation of God in Jesus Christ, attested by Scripture. And it reminds us that the church's confession in various times and places must never be isolated from the fullness of faith confessed by the one, holy, catholic, and apostolic church, which no particular tradition fully embodies. That, in the final analysis, is the essence of ecumenicity and the meaning of catholic Christianity.

The New Testament is well aware of the fact that the church is a child of time and space. It never loses sight of the continuity of the church with the life and history of Israel. Theologians of the church up to and including those of the Protestant Reformation, as well as many theologians today, understand the church in the context of the time process. The church has a past that includes memorable events believed to be foundational and normative for the self-understanding of the contemporary community. Just as the events of the American Revolution, and personages such as George Washington and Thomas Jefferson, are viewed as foundational and determinative for the contemporary life of America, so the church is informed by the memory of the exodus and the Sinai experience, by the memory of the life, teaching, death, and resurrection of Jesus of Nazareth, and by the gift of the Holy Spirit at Pentecost. Just as these events in the history of the United States are rehearsed and reenacted annually in the life of the nation, the church participates in its past through its memory of the past in the present. In its worship and teaching, in its pastoral care and its decision-making processes, the church repeats and interprets the events of the past that it considers to be normative for the present. The story of the church is told in such a way as to enable men and women living in the present to claim the story of the church as their own, to sense their own place and participation in that which happened back then, and to appropriate the story as the story of their lives. When a church, like other human institutions, lives entirely in and for the present moment, separated from the past, it is a sick church. It contracts amnesia, a loss of memory, and loses its sense of direction. The humanity of the church is no more clearly evident than in the fact of its dependence upon a remembered and living past for its present orientation and health.

The processes by which a human institution keeps alive a historical memory, however, are far from simple. They too are radically historical: children of time and space, subject to error, and in constant need of modification and change. These processes involve people, language, symbols, ceremonies and rites, forms and structures of communication and organization. The normative events of the past are interpreted in the present by means of reason, logic, and language. Events are summarized in doctrines, creeds, scriptures, hymns, prayers, and liturgies. These forms seek not only to recall what happened in the past but to interpret what was really going on in what happened as seen through eyes of faith. These summaries of events help the church to keep alive its historical memory and provide the church with its means of communication and transmission.

Furthermore, since the church is a child of time, it attends to these matters of memory, communication, and transmission in the context of the larger world of which it is a part. The church lives in a culture that is either accepting, apathetic, or hostile, and must do its remembering, its communicating, and its transmitting in relation to the particular environment in which it is set. Therefore, although many of the forms of the church's historical memory are maintained and cherished from generation to generation, it is quite likely that much of what the church does in one time will have to be adapted if not changed altogether for another historical time. Reformation of the church is always a double process of a normative past making its claim on people in the present, and of a contemporary environment pressing its claims on the inherited past in transforming and clarifying ways.

Reformation is a renewed subjective understanding of past meanings as they enlighten present issues, and of the actions that are consequent from this.[14] Reformation is the process of reclaiming the past in the present and recovering its meaning in the light of contemporary issues and events. Without ongoing reformation, institutions cease to be relevant to the contemporary needs of people. Reformation in the church, like that in other social organizations, is an essential ingredient for its continued health and viability as a human institution. Each generation requires a renewed understanding of the center of meaning, Jesus Christ, if the church is to maintain its unique identity as a human community.

The church as a child of time and space recalls and interprets its past, and thus identifies itself in the present, in many ways. It does so most graphically, perhaps, in its forms of worship. James Gustafson suggests that this process of recall and interpretation lies at the very heart of the sacraments, and especially of the Lord's Supper.[15] In the sacrament of the Lord's Supper, Christians participate in a dramatic representation of the history of salvation, focused and fulfilled in Jesus Christ. The institution of the Lord's Supper by Jesus Christ is rehearsed, the relationship between the elements and the death of Christ is recalled, and contemporary Christians are invited to participate in the present moment in a communion of people of all times and places. The church of the present, in a real sense, is reconstituted and renewed as the meaning of its formative events is applied to and appropriated by the faith of believers. The Lord's Supper recalls and interprets the center of meaning, Jesus Christ, who gives to the church its unique identity and creates and sustains its social cohesion.

Finally, the church as a child of time and space faces the question of order or chaos in its own institutional life, as other human institutions do. The church is a congregation of men and women who have borne identical and different needs who share the same historical time yet bring with them divergent histories. It is an institution that organizes its life in some form or fashion in order to avoid the chaos of competing wills, needs, and goals. It establishes procedures and processes for the recruitment and training of its leadership in order that its mission might be accomplished today and its transmission secured for tomorrow. Like all social organizations, the church requires a polity or form of government, a ministry of one description or another, and certain political processes for getting things done. These forms and structures of the visible church must reflect and not deny the center of meaning that unites the church and gives to it its unique identity. In the succeeding chapters, therefore, we shall continue our discussion of the humanity of the church by looking at how the church organizes itself and lives in the light of what the church believes.

THE HUMANITY OF THE CHURCH: LIMITED BY TEMPTATION AND SIN

The humanity of the church is perhaps most clearly visible in its capacity for failure. The church as a human institution is limited, like all other human institutions, by its incapacity to embody the reality it represents without mistake, error, distortion, or contradiction. The gospel by which the church is constituted is given by Christ as his pure, genuine, authentic gift. "But from the pure hands of its Lord," the gift passes into the hands of people "united in the community whose creaturely limitation and sinful fallibility make it very doubtful what will become of it."[16] In every age and circumstance, the gospel has been compromised by the fact that the church is human, vulnerable to temptation, and composed of ordinary people who are implicated in sin. The limitation of the church may be seen in five of its most serious temptations: the temptation to kill the gospel, to change the gospel, to trivialize the gospel, to clericalize the gospel, and to con-

ceive of itself as a community of the moral elite. We shall examine each temptation briefly.

First, the church is always tempted to kill the gospel by making of it something fixed and static, a brace of doctrines to be accepted and believed, a system
of timeless truths by which people explain things that are otherwise inexplicable,
something to possess and admire like Longfellow. The temptation of the church
is to become like the Cambridge ladies of whom e e cummings wrote:

> the Cambridge ladies who live in furnished souls
> are unbeautiful and have comfortable minds
> (also, with the church's protestant blessings
> daughters, unscented shapeless spirited)
> they believe in Christ and Longfellow, both dead,
> are invariably interested in so many things—
> at the present writing one still finds
> delighted fingers knitting for the is it Poles?
> perhaps. While permanent faces coyly bandy
> scandal of Mrs. N and Professor D
> . . . the Cambridge ladies do not care, above
> Cambridge if sometimes in its box of
> sky lavender and cornerless, the
> moon rattles like a fragment of angry candy.[17]

The temptation of the church is to institutionalize the gospel, to lose the over-
againstness of it all, to slip out from under its searching judgment and stringent
requirement, and to take from it that unsettling and critical invasion of all com-
placency that gives to it its peculiar ethical bite. When the church falls victim to
this temptation, the gospel of Christ is distorted almost beyond recognition. The
form of religion is maintained, but the force of the gospel is lost. Prayers for peace
may be offered, but they impinge on no one's life. Hymns may be sung, but their
call to decision and discipleship elicits no practical response. Love may be honored in faith, but lives remain unchanged in fact. The world easily tolerates this
kind of church. Opposition is incurred only when the church lives as a people
who are constantly confronted and called to account by the living God.

Second, the church is tempted to change the gospel, to make it more relevant
and up to date, to substitute current insights from the social sciences for the revelation of God, or to confuse ecclesial self-interest with Christian ethics. Sometimes the church appears to be embarrassed by its gospel and ashamed of its
history. It concludes that its language and convictions are old, tired, and irrelevant to the contemporary world. It wears such an obvious hair shirt for the sins
of the past that it can no longer celebrate the providence of God in which even
its sins were used for good. When such is the dominant mood, the temptation is
to bring the gospel up to date and make it relevant. Insights are sought in the culture at large that when coupled to familiar faith categories, construct a decep-
tively new gospel of health, adjustment, integration, and social harmony. The
new gospel traffics in issues more than ideas. It has more to say about social problems than faith problems. It is more comfortable in situations where mental

health concerns or political strategies are being discussed than those in which men and women ask after matters of life and death. Like the temptation to kill the gospel, the temptation to change the gospel amounts to a refusal to be confronted by a living God, an attempt to escape the searching presence of One who seeks not to be relevant but to be trusted and obeyed.

Third, the church is tempted to trivialize the gospel by identifying it with the institution, or earthen vessel, by which it is proclaimed. The church trivializes the gospel when it focuses its attention on itself, its financial success or failure, and its operating procedure. When the church falls victim to this temptation, ministers tend to see themselves as religious professionals, management specialists, and corporate executives. Denominational offices, ecclesiastical bureaucracies, and processes of planning, budgeting, and evaluation become objects of ultimate concern. In 1975, John Fry published a book, *The Trivialization of the United Presbyterian Church*, which stung the officialdom of the denomination and was roundly criticized. The book left itself open to criticism in many places, but it also spoke the truth to church power. It underscored the unwillingness of the members of the bureaucracy to listen to the voice of the people or, having listened, to hear. It pointed to "the global significance of brass tacks" syndrome, whereby reorganization and restructure of the institution assume inordinate significance. Organizational goals are equated with the content of the faith and the accomplishment of these goals with the reformation of the church. Commenting on the reorganization of the United Presbyterian Church, Fry sought to discover why and how such trivialization of the gospel came about.

> This was the reason: the reorganization effort had begun to assume a life of its own. It had become a "religious" activity alongside the denomination's religion. It had the "mission." The people involved in making the reorganization proposals were dedicated to installing a particular kind of organization, with a particular planning emphasis. They were not dummies, aimlessly fastening onto trivial details; they were card-carrying zealots. What gives trivialization its flavor, then, is not its rigid little-mindedness but its very purposiveness.[18]

Things have not changed very much, at least in this regard, since Fry wrote his troublesome book. Reorganization of church structures may or may not serve the mission that the church is called to perform. But when institutional structures and forms are equated with the mission of the church, the gospel of God is always trivialized.

Fourth, the church is tempted to clericalize the gospel by allowing itself and its mission to be identified with the work of its clergy and by granting to them virtual hegemony over the church's form and function. It is not certain when the church first fell victim to this temptation. Very early the church came under the control of persons of recognized knowledge and competence in the apostolic tradition. Clerical domination of the church was established as early as the beginning of the second century. The case was made for apostolic succession in the fourth quarter of the second century by Irenaeus, and it was not long thereafter that Cyprian, bishop of Carthage, insisted that bishops were necessary not only for the administrative well-being (*bene esse*) but for the very existence (*esse*) of the church. Although lay groups were organized around the various trades in the Middle Ages, no one would deny that by then both the gospel and the church were held firmly in the hands of the clergy. The Protestant Reformation sought to liberate the church from its "Babylonian Captivity" to the clergy. Luther spoke of the priesthood of all believers, and Calvin sought to recover the significance of the local congregation as the basic unit of Christian faith and life. Neither fully succeeded. Lutheran polity continued to depend on the established power of the clergy and the princes, and Calvin's churchmanship was grounded in such strict discipline that congregational life was far from spontaneous and free from clerical control. The Anabaptist movement of the seventeenth century may have done more than either to break the stranglehold of clericalism on the church by emphasizing the warmth and joy of life in the Christian congregation.

The church exists in many places, but the clearest manifestation of the church is the local congregation, where the Word is preached, the sacraments administered, and people try to live in love and charity with their neighbors. Reformed Christians seek to defend against the temptation to clericalism by giving expression to the ministry of the laity, by providing for parity between clergy and laity in the polity, and by asserting the right and duty of a people to elect their own officers and ministers. The tragedy is that, even so, the system breaks down. Laypersons have only a limited amount of time to give to the affairs of the institutional church, while ministers are in its full-time employ. Few laypersons have the time to become familiar with the intricacies of the institution. Consequently, they tend to become discouraged at their inability to make the system work for them, and thus they create a leadership vacuum that ministers are not reluctant to fill. This may be inevitable and necessary at times due to practical circumstances, but clericalism always distorts the gospel and cripples the church. There is but one essential ministry of the church, the ministry of its living Lord, in which all members, laity as well as clergy, are given an equal share. Any distinctions beyond distinctions of vocation made between the laity and the clergy obscure the fact that, although there are varieties of service, it is the same Spirit who inspires them all for the common good.

Fifth, the church is tempted to conceive of itself, and thus to live, as a community of the moral elite. The famous Pelagian controversy in the fifth century, which set Augustine over against Pelagius and his followers, is usually defined as a controversy over the relationship between the freedom of the will and the efficacy of God's grace. It was that, but it was more than that. The Pelagian controversy was a controversy over the nature of the church and, as such, it bears witness to the church's humanity. Pelagius was a British monk, a layman of great intelligence, who lived an austere, ascetic life. Having come from Britain to Rome at the very end of the fourth century, Pelagius was scandalized by the loose living of the Roman populace and sought to persuade them to reform their lives. Pelagius was a social activist, a reformer, who could not tolerate imperfection. He felt that a person at birth has the ability to choose good over evil, that there is no such thing as original sin or any other kind of determinism that relieves a person from responsibility for his or her life. Pelagius felt that people could be perfect as God is perfect, that the law of God could be obeyed by people who willed to obey it, and that there is little or no place in the church for moral failure.

Augustine opposed the Pelagians on at least three grounds. First, Augustine was profoundly convinced of the essential unity of the human race. He felt that the church should manifest that unity and resist every temptation to exclusivity. He felt that the church must be careful not to categorize people into the good and the bad, the desirable and the undesirable. He believed that the mission of the church is to bring people together, not to tear them apart. Second, Augustine took the reality of sin more seriously than did Pelagius. For Pelagius, sin was real but superficial, a bad moral choice, a personality disorder. A modern Pelagian might treat sin as maladjustment, emotional instability, or even mental illness, and recommend psychotherapy as a cure. For Augustine, the situation was much more complex than that. He felt that men and women are victims of a permanent dislocation of the soul. People want health and seek health, but even their wanting and seeking are distorted beyond all human capacities to heal. Pelagius believed that a person can be good if he or she really tries. Augustine, on the other hand, felt that people are trapped by sin, which, long before Sigmund Freud, he called "the constant activity of unconscious desires." Augustine sensed the pathos of the human condition, perhaps because it was no academic matter for him personally, struggling as he did against the onslaught of sexual lust. He wrote, "For many sins are committed through pride; but yet not all things which are wrongly done are done proudly,—at any rate, not by the ignorant, not by the infirm, and not, generally speaking, by the weeping and the sorrowful."[19] Third, Augustine believed that the church is a healing community, a community of love and forgiveness, in which men and women participate in a lifelong process of growth in grace.

> Augustine's audience . . . would be told repeatedly that even the baptized Christian must remain an invalid. Like the wounded man, found near death by the wayside in the Parable of the Good Samaritan, his life had been saved by the rite of baptism; but he must be content to endure, for the rest of his life, a prolonged and precarious convalescence in the "Inn" of the Church. [20]

According to Augustine, the church is not for good people but for sinners all, more nearly comparable to a hospital than to a society of the morally elite.

It has been suggested that the difference between Augustine and Pelagius can be illustrated by their attitudes toward babies.[21] Augustine loved babies and was impressed by the extent of their helplessness. He likened his relationship to God to that of a baby at its mother's breast, utterly dependent on the mother as the source of life. Pelagius, on the other hand, was not fond of babies. He felt that people are called to be mature sons and daughters of God, independent of their parents, living in their own power to determine good from evil. Pelagius was a man of northern temperament, a severe logician, a clear, calm, imaginative thinker, who lived from childhood the peaceful life of a monk. Augustine, on the other hand, was a man of many thunderstorms: a sensualist, a doubter, hot-blooded, whose whole life had been spent in struggle with himself and his enemies. Augustine stood against the temptation to moralize the gospel of God's grace and for the inclusiveness of the church.

Whenever the church is tempted to select certain forms of human behavior, to label them as sin, to categorize people accordingly, and to purify itself by excluding the sinner from participation or prominence in the church, it needs to recall who it is as the beneficiary and the bearer of God's unconditional and forgiving grace. Of the five temptations that beset the church as a human community today, none is more treacherous than the temptation to turn the church into a community of the moral elite. Self-righteousness has always been the besetting sin of the church. Jesus was not harassed and finally killed by the people who were deemed to be sinners by the religious folk of the time. Jesus was done in by the self-proclaimed righteous people, who had little sense of their own sin and little need for a Savior. Reformed Christians at their best know that God expects them to live moral lives, but they know with even more certainty that they are sinners and that the church is a community of grace, an imperfect people with many spots and blemishes, whose only hope is the grace and mercy of God.

THE SPIRIT OF REFORM
AND THE REFORMED SPIRIT

Whenever Reformed people speak of the Spirit of the church, they speak of none other than the judging, reforming, renewing Spirit of the living God, made known in Jesus Christ. The church belongs to God. It is the creature of God's creative Word. The church's ancient story is God's story, apart from which the church is nothing. God loves the church, refuses to give up on the church, and is always present to the church through the Spirit. But the Spirit by whom God sustains the church in being is not an easy Spirit, who sanctifies all that the visible church is and does. Quite the contrary, judgment begins with the household of God (1 Pet. 4:17). The humanity of the church is such that it never encompasses the will and work of God once and for all. The church is a responding people, whose responses are always partial and imperfect, dependent on justification from on high, candidates for redemption and renewal. Therefore, the Spirit of God present to the church is the Spirit of reform, who is constantly at work in the church and in all of its historical forms to recreate the church into a more adequate vehicle of God's will and work.

God remains the same from one generation to the next. But the church can never remain static, hard, inflexible, or fixed. The church must always be on the move and in the process of change if it is to be adequate for the time. It must always remain open to the reforming activity of God's Spirit in all of its institutional life.

The recovery of the spirit of reform was one of the great contributions of the Protestant Reformation. In faithfulness to the center of meaning that gives it its unique identity, the church said No to itself. From within itself, Reformers arose who dared to oppose the institution they loved and served until finally their ideas became the conviction of others and the institution itself was changed. The tragedy is that people sometimes consider the reformation of the church to be over and done with, a datable event in the sixteenth century that need never be repeated again. The truth of the matter is that the essence of the sixteenth-century Reformation was faithfulness to the gospel in the life of the church. That must happen time and time again in every generation. The reformation of the church must go on and never stop. Until the kingdom comes "on earth as it is in heaven," the church as a human community will always be in need of reform. The church will need men and women whose faithfulness to the gospel can be used of the Spirit as an instrument of continuing reformation.

The Reformed spirit, which exists not only in Reformed communities but in every congregation, denomination, or ecumenical event where the spirit of reform is at work, has often been summarized by four Latin words: *ecclesia reformata semper reformanda,* the church reformed but always reforming. That summary of the Reformed spirit contains at least three affirmations of faith. First, it contains the implicit assumption that God is sovereign, that Christ is Lord, and that one's total allegiance can be given to nothing and to no one else—neither family, nor nation, nor church. Second, it affirms that which Paul Tillich called "the Protestant principle," namely, that one must never allow a relative thing to sit on an absolute throne. No human institution, doctrine, book, or relationship is to become an object of ultimate loyalty. Nothing of this world is ever to be treated as though it were divine. Third, it acknowledges that the church must always be open to change in the light of the gospel. It must not be conservative in the sense that it seeks to guarantee its own existence by conserving its own life, but must always remain open to the Spirit of reform as God gives the church new life in every generation.

Chapter 7

The Polity and Politics
of the Church

*The church thus orders its life as an institution with a constitution,
government, officers, finances, and administrative rules. These are
instruments of mission, not ends in themselves. Different orders
have served the gospel, and none can claim exclusive validity. A
Presbyterian polity recognizes the responsibility of all members for
ministry and maintains the organic relation of all congregations in
the church. It seeks to protect the church from exploitation by ecclesiastical or secular power and ambition. Every church order must
be open to such reformation as may be required to make it a more
effective instrument of the mission of reconciliation.*

The Confession of 1967

The church as a human community requires form and order if it is to function
effectively in the world. The church may be a colony of heaven, called into being
and equipped by God to be God's instrument in the renovation of the fallen
world. But the church is like other social groups in that it cannot exist as a viable
human association without structure and organization. Reformed people have
always regarded the polity, or organized life of the church, as a matter of utmost
importance, first, because they believed the polity of the church to be a gift of
God; second, because they believed that the polity was a vehicle of service to God;
and third, because they believed that disciplined life is necessary if the church is
to live with integrity in the world. Furthermore, as Calvin noted, just as no city
or township can function without magistrate and polity, so the church needs a
spiritual polity. Church order is "framed for the preservation of the spiritual
polity."[1] In other words, Calvin and those who followed in his train were quick

to see that "faith cannot be separated from the form in which it expresses itself."[2] The polity of a particular church both reflects and shapes Christian identity. It reflects the reigning theological consensus concerning such things as the nature of the church, the source of authority, the reality of sin, the prospect of salvation, and the content of hope. The polity of a particular church also influences what people believe, since it is within the polity that people worship and learn, celebrate and serve. The form the church takes, for example, either encourages people to religious individualism or to the shared life of the community. Some polities focus the believer's attention on the exalted vision of God, others on the obedience to God in the common life. Thus, polity is a matter of theological as well as practical importance for the life of the church.

TYPES OF REFORMED POLITIES

Reformed people have lived happily under each of the three classic types of church polity: episcopal, congregational, and presbyterian. The episcopal polity (Greek, *episcopos,* "bishop") is government by bishops, duly elected by representatives of the church and consecrated by their fellow bishops. According to Calvin, early in the history of the church, the office of bishop was a functional office, created to meet the need of the times. In each city, presbyters, elected by the people, chose one from their number to whom they gave the title of bishop. The bishop was the chief teacher and administrator, who knew himself to be superior to the other presbyters according to the custom of the church rather than by Christ's decree.[3] Later, the episcopacy acquired new meaning. Bishops increasingly were regarded as central to the existence of the church, necessary for ordination as well as confirmation, with apostolic succession being the guarantor of continuity with the past. Reformed people share this conviction that the church is one. Reformed communities have lived at times under the episcopal order, especially when the emphasis has been placed on an administrative and pastoral, rather than an essential, episcopacy. Reformed theology, however, has never been compatible with the later development of a theological or sacramental episcopacy. The Hungarian Reformed Church today lives under an episcopal polity, but the bishops in that church clearly have a functional, not an essential or constitutive significance.

Congregational polity is based on an understanding of the church as a "gathered community," that is, a free association of believers in Christ, which vests ecclesiastical authority in the local congregation. In this polity, the locus of responsibility for church order is the congregational meeting, where all members have the opportunity to discuss and vote on matters concerning the particular church. Congregationalism developed as a part of the so-called free church movement, which came into being in the face of oppression by established churches. Members of the free church movement wanted to worship and to preach as they felt they should without coercion or direction from ecclesiastical authority. Their history is a history of considerable persecution and suffering. Free church theology was Calvinist to the core and gave rise to the Puritan movement in Great Britain in the sixteenth century. English Congregationalists were originally members of the Church of England who broke with the creedal posture and traditions of the established church in order to purify their worship on the basis of strict adherence to Scripture. They sought to base their church order on the practices of the early church as recorded in the New Testament, emphasizing the autonomy of the local congregation, the operation of the Holy Spirit in the free association of believers, and the holiness of life lived by the individual Christian. Reformed people have always had much in common with this view of the church, and especially with the fierce independence of those who have held it. Reformed communities have lived happily under the congregational polity, both in Great Britain and in the United States.

For the most part, however, Reformed people have identified themselves with presbyterian polity (Greek, *presbuteros,* "elder"), which is government by elders elected by the people to serve in representative assemblies of regular gradation. The principles of presbyterian polity, later expressed in the governing forms of particular churches, were given their classical expression in the *Ecclesiastical Ordinances* for John Calvin's church in Geneva, adopted in 1541. Calvin knew that no church could prosper, or even exist for very long as a viable human association, without some form of government. The exercise of power in the medieval church was that against which the Reformers felt called to protest. They saw little hope for the reformation of doctrine under the rule of existing church hierarchy. Thus, they sought a form of church order that would be a vehicle for evangelical truth and provide a congenial context for the birth and growth of faith. As Eugene Osterhaven explains, "In doing this they succeeded to a degree beyond their fondest expectations and their success, in the Calvinistic part of the Reformation at least, was due in large measure to the new organization of the church and its ministry."[4]

Calvin believed that the government of the church was administered by Jesus Christ, the head of the church, and that he should have all authority and preeminence in it. Nevertheless, because Christ does not now dwell among us in visible form, he has chosen to use "the ministry of men to declare openly his will to us by mouth, as a sort of delegated work, not by transferring to them his right and honor, but only that through their mouths he may do his own work—just as a workman uses a tool to do his work."[5] The *Ecclesiastical Ordinances* specify that Christ instituted four offices: pastors, doctors, elders, and deacons, in order that the church may be well ordered and maintained.

Pastors are to preach the Word of God, instruct, admonish, administer the sacraments, and, with the elders, exercise discipline. Candidates for this office must give evidence of their calling, first by passing an examination in theology and by being approved in conduct; second, by being accepted by one's peers and by the Little Council of Geneva; and third, by receiving the consent of the people whom the pastor is to serve. "As to the manner of introducing him, it is good to use the imposition of hands, which ceremony was observed by the apostles and then in the ancient Church, providing that it take place without superstition and without offense."[6]

Doctors, or teachers, are to instruct the faithful in true doctrine, that the purity of the gospel be not corrupted either by ignorance or by contrary opinions. They are to equip the church to maintain the apostolic faith and to defend it from injury by default of the pastors. "The degree nearest to the minister and most closely joined to the government of the Church is the lecturer in theology, of which it will be good to have one in Old Testament and one in New Testament."[7]

Recent discussions of the importance of the ministry of the laity have called into question the use of the definite article before the word *ministry.* It is often argued, and rightly so, that every Christian is called of God to a life of faith and service, and commissioned for this task at the time of baptism. In the broadest sense of the term, the ministry of the church is one to which each Christian is called of God. Therefore, no one person should be referred to as "the minister," and no one group should be called ministers, since all Christians are ministers of Jesus Christ.

There is much to be said for this clarification of our understanding of Christian vocation. H. Richard Niebuhr suggested that each person is called to be a Christian. Each person is called to discipleship in Christ, to the hearing and doing of the Word of God, to repentance and faith. Some people, however, are claimed by the secret call, namely, the inner persuasion of experience whereby one feels directly summoned or invited by God to take up the ministry of the Word and sacraments; by the providential call, which is the invitation and command to take up this ministry that comes to a person through the possession of talents necessary for the office and through a sense of divine guidance of one's life to this end; and by the ecclesiastical call, whereby the church validates the secret and providential call, and invites or summons the individual to undertake the ministry of the Word and sacraments within a particular community.[8]

The Reformers would have agreed with Niebuhr's understanding of the call. Martin Luther, who, as we have seen, explicated the doctrine of the universal priesthood most clearly, asserted that there is a distinction to be made between the priesthood of all believers and the ministry of the Word and sacraments in particular. John Calvin assumed, but spent little time defining, the secret call.

> I pass over that secret call, of which each minister is conscious before God, and which does not have the church as witness. But there is the good witness of our heart that we receive the proffered office not with ambition or avarice, not with any other selfish desire, but with a sincere fear of God and desire to build up the church.[9]

Calvin believed that the call of a minister is in accord with the Word of God when those who seem fit are confirmed by the consent and approval of the church. However, it would be to misunderstand Calvin to assert that the secret and providential call were matters of insignificance in his understanding of the ministry. Calvin believed that each individual "has his own kind of living assigned to him by the Lord as a sort of sentry post so that he may not heedlessly wander about throughout life." He calls these various kinds of living "callings," and we may be sure that he did not exclude the ministry of the Word and sacraments from his high view of Christian vocation. "From this will arise also a singular consolation," Calvin wrote, "that no task will be so sordid and base, provided you obey your calling in it, that it will not shine and be reckoned very precious in God's sight."[10] That which holds good for all callings holds good all the more for the Christian ministry. When the conviction of God's secret and providential call to the function of the ministry of Word and sacraments is lost, and the ministry is understood primarily in professional terms, the integrity of the church is compromised. On the other hand, when ministers view even the most routine, mundane tasks of building and nurturing the congregations they serve as tasks that are "very precious in God's sight," the church is strengthened at the sinews of its life for the service of God and neighbor.

The reticence to claim that some people are called of God to particular functions in the ministry of the church is occasioned not only by a misunderstanding of the call but by confusion concerning what is meant by the word *office*. Emil Brunner has noted that it is a mistake to translate the Greek word *diakonia* by "offices."[11] The word refers to ministries or functions of ministry. Once it is claimed that certain people are established in office by God, a divinely ordained ecclesiastical structure emerges wherein certain people wield power by divine right, and a cleavage is opened between clergy and laity that was never intended in the apostolic church. "We must win through to a conception of the office of the clergy as service," Brunner writes, "which can be so exercised that the whole congregation is drawn in to share responsibility and share in the work according to its gifts and powers."[12]

The Reformed doctrine of the church affirms that, though all members are ministers in the broad sense of the term, certain people are called and equipped by God for specific callings, such as pastor or teacher. Christ's gifts were "that some would be apostles, some prophets, some evangelists, some pastors and teachers, to the saints for the work of ministry, for building up the body of Christ" (Eph. 4:11–12). The distinction between the ministry of all and the ministry of Word and sacrament is one of vocation, not one of theological preeminence or spiritual superiority. The Second Helvetic Confession sums the matter up as follows:

> To be sure, Christ's apostles call all who believe in Christ "priests," but not on account of an office, but because, all the faithful having been made kings and priests, we are able to offer up spiritual sacrifices to God through Christ. . . . Therefore, the priesthood and the ministry are very different from one another. For the priesthood, as we have said, is common to all Christians; not so is the ministry. Nor have we abolished the ministry of the Church because we have repudiated the papal priesthood from the Church of Christ.[13]

The office of elder was fundamental to Calvin's Genevan polity, as it has been in Reformed churches since that time. G. D. Henderson has noted that the Reformation not only involved great anticlerical sentiment, but that laypersons played an important role in the movement. "Political leaders like Admiral Coligny and William the Silent, Philip of Hesse, the Regent Moray and Henry VIII, scholars and thinkers like de Berquin in France, Melanchthon in Germany, Aonio Paleario in Italy, but perhaps above all the stout citizens and shrewd merchants of Northern Europe, decided the issue."[14] The Basel Reformer, John Oecolampadius, first made an attempt to institute an eldership independent of civil authority to exercise discipline in the church, whereas before ecclesiastical authority was lodged in the civil magistrate. Oecolampadius's views influenced John Calvin, who after prolonged conflict in Geneva finally instituted a scheme of lay discipline that became the model for Reformed churches. The *Ecclesiastical Ordinances* reflect Calvin's conviction that the Christian community not only hears and believes God's Word but that it also lives to God's glory. Therefore, it calls for the office of elder "to have oversight of the life of everyone, to admonish amicably those whom they see to be erring or to be living a disordered life, and, where it is required, to enjoin fraternal corrections themselves and along with others."[15] These elders, elected so that there should be representatives from every quarter of the city "to keep an eye on everybody," should be "men of good and honest life, without reproach and beyond suspicion, and above all fearing God and possessing spiritual prudence."[16] The office of elder was regarded as a spiritual office, elders not being called ministers, yet being recognized as exercising a valid and important ministry in and for the church.

The office of deacon was of two kinds: those deputed to receive, dispense, and hold goods for the poor, "not only daily alms, but also possessions, rents and pensions; the other to tend and care for the sick and administer allowances to the poor."[17] John Calvin and those who shared his theological convictions recognized the church's essential and direct responsibility in relation to social issues. The giving of alms to the poor, he believed, was a Christian duty, which ought not to be given over to the state. The blessings that Christians enjoy are divine trusts to be used for the benefit of the neighbor and to be dispensed in accord with the law of love. Thus, Calvin regarded the office of deacon as a ministry instituted by Christ, not merely for the city of Geneva with its hospital and begging problems, its widowed, orphans, and aged infirm, but as a permanent ministry in the organized church.

PRINCIPLES OF PRESBYTERIAN POLITY

If it is true that the Reformed faith cannot be separated from the polity in which it finds expression, that faith both shapes and is shaped by the order of the church's life, then it will profit us here to try to identify the underlying principles of Presbyterian polity.

First, the authority of the Bible. Presbyterians have always sought to conform church order to Scripture, looking to Scripture both for the justification of institutional forms and for the forms themselves. At times, Presbyterians have claimed to have the only scriptural form of church government, though most people today do not seriously believe that the Bible sets forth only one true polity. Presbyterians affirm that other polities than their own may also be in accord with Scripture. Nevertheless, they believe that Presbyterian polity is in accord with Scripture; that it admits to the sovereignty of God, the Lordship of Christ, and the activity of the Holy Spirit; that it recognizes the need for personal faith and individuality over against routinization and superstition; that it emphasizes the calling of the laity, stresses the ethical significance of sanctification, underscores a distrust of power, and suggests a readiness for intercommunion; and that, above all, it insists on the priority of the Word of God in Christian faith and life.

Second, the subordination of the polity to the gospel. Reformed Christians have never believed that the polity of the church determines the existence of the church. The only thing that determines the existence of the church is the gospel. Speaking of the form and laws in church constitutions, Calvin noted, "They are not to be considered necessary for salvation and thus bind consciences by scruples; nor are they to be associated with the worship of God, and piety thus be lodged in them. . . . For here nothing is required except that love be fostered among us by common effort."[18]

Third, the unity of the church. We have already discussed the essential unity of the church in chapter 4. It is important to note here that Presbyterians manifest and participate in that unity through a series of judicatories or church courts, composed of ministers and elders. These representative assemblies are the session, the presbytery, the synod, and the General Assembly. Through these assemblies, people work together on tasks that individually they could not undertake, and participate with other Christians in ecumenical councils and consortia in their own region, country, and throughout the world.

Fourth, the place of the layperson in spiritual affairs. Presbyterian polity assumes that vocation is universal, that people have different functions or ministries to perform in the life of the church, and that ordained offices are representative of the ministry of the whole church. Furthermore, Presbyterians intend a parity of elders. No elder, minister, or ruling elder is spiritually superior to another in the polity of the church. Both ministers and elders may chair committees or serve as moderators of church judicatories, and all positions of responsibility are normally held for a limited period of time.

Fifth, the freedom of the individual conscience. Presbyterians have long been convinced that, though we be subject to one another in Christ, God alone is lord of the conscience and that the commandments and doctrines of churches dare not bind the conscience in matters of faith and worship. They have claimed the right of individual judgment in all matters that respect religion to be universal and inalienable.

Sixth, the right of the people to elect their own officers and to choose their own minister. G. D. Henderson quotes Tom Jones as having said, "I don't care what religion comes; provided the Presbyterians are not uppermost; for they are enemies to puppet-shows."[19] Presbyterians have always objected when a church judicatory or self-styled bishop sought to tamper with the right of the people to elect officers and to call a minister. They have done so on the basis of the conviction that God's will is best discerned by representative assemblies rather than by even the most prayerful deliberation of any single individual or small executive group.

Other things might well be included in this brief summary of underlying principles of Presbyterian polity, but these will be sufficient to suggest the milieu in which most Reformed communities live.

THE CHURCH
AS A VOLUNTARY ASSOCIATION

The Form of Government of the Presbyterian Church (U.S.A.) contains an assumption that may not deserve the status of a principle of Presbyterian polity but nevertheless is crucial to its proper functioning: "The organization rests on the fellowship and is not designed to work without trust and love." In other words, the church as a human community is a voluntary association, without benefit of police power and thus without means to coerce its membership into believing or acting in a particular way. The only power that church leaders have is the power of suasion in the context of an organization that rests on the fellowship and is not designed to work without trust and love.

How are trust and love nurtured and preserved within the polity of the church? The answer to this question comes with an understanding of the significance of the church as a voluntary association. Churches in the United States are voluntary associations by law. Freedom of religion is basic to the Constitution of the United States. But even in those countries where membership is conferred on a person at birth, personal commitment to Jesus Christ and devotion to the church are still voluntary. A congregation may carry a person's name on its roll without his or her consent if it so desires, but no church can force that person to trust Christ as Lord and Savior and to love the neighbor as the self. Church membership, in any sense that really matters, is a voluntary affair. Even Reformed churches that hold to an exalted view of infant baptism, believing that baptized children are also members of the church, are nonetheless voluntary associations. At maturity, the person baptized in infancy must confirm the faith in which he or she was baptized or else church membership will mean little to that person. Churches that practice only adult baptism may see this more clearly than those that practice infant baptism, although those practicing only adult baptism may miss seeing important things about church membership. The point is that church membership, humanly speaking, is voluntary, requiring personal decision at some point to be effective.

Reformed churches in the United States today are very different in this respect from the "gathered church" of the Puritan era.[20] We no longer have anything like the kind of clarity of definition concerning who is a member of the church and who is not that existed in the gathered church idea. The Puritan gathered church laid out three tests for church membership: the evangelical experience of redeeming grace, orthodox belief, and righteous behavior in everyday life. The Puritans believed that God's elect would manifest their election in daily life, making it clear who was inside and who was outside the circle of the church. The gathered church, however, has evolved into the voluntary church. The decisive criterion for church membership today is not "experienced predestination," the activity of the Christian in the world that marks his or her election, but simply the will to belong.[21] The Puritan quest for the purity of the church has long since given way to the concept of an open membership, except in certain sects of conservative Protestantism. Instead of the idea of the gathered church, understood as people elected by God and gathered together as a group distinct from all the rest, the church today gives the appearance of being a loosely knit company of individuals who decide of their own free will to identify with the church because it promises to meet their needs or offers them a vehicle for service.

The emergence of the volunteer church has resulted in new bases for church membership. We speak today of the parish and of parish ministry, and in so doing we betray the fact that we have not fully understood what has happened to the American church in recent years. At one time, the parish church delineated church membership in geographical terms. People lived geographically in one parish or another, over which the parish church and the parish minister had spiritual oversight. There is no parish church or ministry in modern America, and church membership is no longer defined by geographical boundaries alone. Sometimes people do join the church in their neighborhood, but even then it is their choice to do so. No congregation today would presume that a person belongs to that church simply because the person resides in its neighborhood. The will to belong, humanly speaking, is by far the most significant basis of church membership today. Likewise, few congregations exclude people from their membership on the basis of an inadequate experience of regeneration, a difference in doctrine, or an error in judgment or behavior.

Furthermore, prospective church members freely choose the church to which they will belong. People "shop around" for a church in typical free enterprise fashion. They may decide to join a particular church because of the beauty of its liturgy or the architecture of the building, because they like the preaching, or because the members are friendly. The social place and prestige of a denomination or a local congregation may coincide with the self-image of a prospective member or with the desire for upward mobility. Racial and ethnic factors may also be important in a person's decision to join a church. People of a certain ethnic background may choose a church that promises to nurture that particular ethnic identity. African American people, until recently, had no other option than to join racially segregated churches. Even now, however, when most churches are open to people of all races, racial minorities may elect to associate with a church that promises to maintain their particular racial identity. The point is that the gathered church idea and the parish church model are essentially dead in the

United States. People no longer define their church membership in terms of their election by God from among the rest, their call to come out and be separate, or their identity as a geographical parish. Reformed communities, like other religious communities, are highly voluntary associations. "The consequence of this development is that people are freer to be or not to be Christian than they have been in many places in the West since the fifth century."[22] The leaders of these churches must come to terms with this fact if they are to be effective in building, sustaining, and nourishing an organization that is based on fellowship and that is not designed to work without trust and love.

One of the negative aspects of a voluntary church is that it tends to become a homogeneous social group. Presbyterian churches in America are sometimes criticized for being one-class churches, and there is good reason for such criticism. The patterns of life that bring people together and form interpersonal bonds of unity are naturally carried over into the lives of churches. Educational levels, economic conditions, and residential patterns combine to bring like people together in like places, open to them similar opportunities for work and recreation, and provide for them homogeneous churches. This sociological reality presents a theological problem for the church. Homogeneous churches easily become comfortable social groups that reinforce existing values of life. Ministers may be tempted to defend themselves from the critique of the gospel, and to spare their people from it as well, in order to maintain harmony. Laypersons may be tempted to equate existing values and ways of life with the content of the Christian faith.

The antidote for this, of course, is the heterogenous church. Christian faith affirms that all people are made one in Christ. This conviction should impel churches toward greater inclusiveness. But heterogeneity is no panacea for the problems of the church as a voluntary community. Heterogeneity has its own set of problems, not the least of which is the basis for membership. It soon becomes apparent in a heterogeneous community that the will to belong in and of itself is an inadequate basis for membership. People who are otherwise very different from each other must share common commitments or loyalties that transcend and qualify the will to belong if they are to be held together in a heterogeneous social group. These shared commitments or loyalties may be to a certain liturgy, or to a particular creedal posture, or to some historical tradition, such as the Reformed tradition. Whatever they be, these transcending commitments and loyalties must be capable of providing a unifying center of cohesiveness that is able to hold people together in spite of their differences.

Churches determined to strive for greater inclusiveness must be equally committed to producing leaders who are able to communicate and nurture this unifying center of cohesiveness. In so doing, the positive aspects of a homogeneous situation should not be overlooked. A homogeneous church may not have the benefit of diversity in life experience from which to learn, but it is not thereby devoid of possibilities for experiencing and proclaiming the gospel. A homogeneous church offers unique opportunities for understanding between minister and people, and among the people themselves. People in similar walks of life may know each other so well that they are able and free to critique and support each other, to identify common ethical dilemmas, and to sustain each other in ways that only kindred spirits can do. Furthermore, in many one-class churches of the middle and upper middle class, the membership may well include people who exercise considerable influence in the community, such as lawyers, doctors, educators, business executives. This should not be an embarrassment for the church but should be seized and used as an opportunity for evangelism and witness.

When all is said and done, the most difficult problem faced by the voluntary church is the problem of authority. Churches customarily attempt to deal with the problem of authority in one of three ways. Some churches, such as the Roman Catholic Church, vest the institution itself with final authority in faith and morals. The Protestant Reformers, in response to the abuse of authority by the institution, vested Scripture with final authority. Scripture, some have said in derision, is the Protestant paper pope! But biblical scholarship over the past fifty years has called the Bible as a literal authority into question by applying the tools of historical and literary criticism. That which once was considered to be timeless truth has been shown to be the outgrowth of a particular historical time or as the expression of a particular literary form. If authority is not vested in the institution or in the source material of faith, where is the seat of authority in a voluntary church?

The third answer that is often given, especially by the sects, is that the ultimate authority in matters of faith and morals rests in personal religious experience. Authority from all external means, such as an institution or a book, is rejected. Individuals are told to look within themselves for the authentication of faith and the voice of conscience. The authority of human experience, however, may lead to anarchy in the church, since the experience of one is not likely to be identical to the experience of others.

Where then does authority lie in a voluntary association? The legal, psychological, social, and interior pressures that once compelled people to be Christian and to join a church are essentially gone. People choose to participate of their own volition, not because some external force has compelled them. Frequency of attendance, the amount of financial support, and the degree of personal commitment to the doctrine and social proclamations of the church are all matters of private and free decision. If people strongly object to what the church says or does, they are free to join another or to belong to no church at all. How is a social group organized, governed, motivated, and mobilized for action in the absence of any power on the part of the leadership to enforce its decisions?

The answer is that all authority in the church, as in other voluntary associations, is limited authority, granted to those who hold it by the will of the majority of those who belong. The success of any voluntary association depends on the achievement of a basic consensus of the membership on the meaning and purpose of the organization, on the basis of which authority is granted and exercised. As a part of this consensus, the majority of the membership of a voluntary association must generally agree on what holds the group together and what the goals of the group are. From this consensus, individual members derive benefits, such as meaning, purpose, and direction, that sustain their membership in this voluntary group. A person who derives no benefits from the group at all is not likely to continue to participate in it. Not long ago a Gallup poll turned up a statistic of great importance to Presbyterians. Pollsters sought to discover how people feel about the church to which they belong. Ninety-seven percent of Lutherans had positive feelings toward their church, as did 95 percent of Episcopalians and 91 percent of Catholics. Compared to others, Presbyterians showed the lowest self-esteem rating on the charts. Only 48 percent responded positively about their own identity as Presbyterians. Presbyterian churches lost thousands of members in the 1970s and 1980s as a result of internal tension over controversial General Assembly pronouncements.[23] The primary reason for such attrition may not have been the exhibition of singular courage on the part of the leadership but the absence of such theological reflection on their part as might legitimate prophetic action in the mind of the membership.

One of the tasks of leadership in such an organization is to make certain that the voluntary association continues to meet the needs of the membership, conscious of the fact that when any social group ceases to do that, membership will be lost. When church leaders lead effectively, sufficient authority is granted by the membership to accomplish the acknowledged task. When church leaders fail to communicate and nurture a unifying center of cohesiveness, or cease to be accountable to the membership as well as to the claims of the gospel, trust and love are shaken. Authority is either withdrawn or else met by the counterauthority of an alienated membership, and the organization that once was based on the fellowship ceases by design to function as it should. Authority is always limited, proscribed authority in a voluntary association, granted and withdrawn, confirmed or countered, by means of political strategy and activity. Althusius, one of the most systematic of the early Calvinist theorists, said, "Politics is the art of associating ("consociandi") men for the purpose of establishing, cultivating, and conserving social life among them. Whence it is called "symbiotics." The subject matter of politics is therefore association ("consociatio").[24] If politics is the art of associating, and if association is the subject matter of politics, we do well to ask what part politics plays in the granting and exercising of authority in the church as a voluntary association.

THE CHURCH
AS A POLITICAL COMMUNITY

Paul Lehmann tried to recover the word *politics* for theology and the church by taking it out of the hands of secular politicians and restoring it to its original meaning.[25] In the Western cultural tradition, Lehmann tells us, the word *politics* was given its philosophical orientation by the philosophers of ancient Greece, especially Aristotle. According to Aristotle, politics is the science of the highest or supreme Good. "The Good of man," Aristotle said, "must be the end of the science of Politics."[26] Thus, politics has to do with the practical quest for the human good. For Aristotle, politics is the study of the theory and practice of the *polis*, the Greek word for "city" or "city-state," which he considered to be the ideal form of human association, a human community that was necessary for and an expression of the fulfillment of human life. It is instructive to note in this regard that Aristotle uses the same word to refer to the quality of life in the ideal city-state that we met when we discussed the New Testament view of the quality of life in the church, namely, *koinonia*. For Aristotle, koinonia has to do with the shared life of men and women in the context of which they discover and become who they are. Politics is the study or theory of how this ideal form of human association is brought about.

Paul Lehmann speaks of God as Politician. Others have called God the Prime Mover, the First Cause, or a Mathematician. On the basis of the biblical story, Lehmann calls God a Politician in the sense that God is at work creating this ideal form of human association in the midst of the fallen world. God acts in history to draw people into koinonia with himself and with each other, that people might discover and become who they are as children of God. The politics of the church, therefore, should reflect and participate in the politics of God. Polities, constitutions, property, programs, and other institutional forms may thus become instruments of God's renovating activity in the world. The politics of the church cannot be equated with the politics of God. The politics of the church are always vulnerable to the temptations of institutional self-justification and self-preservation. On the other hand, church people need not deny or be embarrassed by the fact that the church as a voluntary association is also a highly political association. Politics is the art of associating, in Althusius's words, the study and the practice of community, the means by which God nurtures and preserves a people. The church in its functioning life is a political community because God is a political God, whose will is human association.

The church constantly reflects on its reason for being, its mission, and its resources. It sets goals and devises strategies to meet those goals. It tries to marshal the resources at its disposal and allocate them in effective ways. It grants authority to certain persons and vests varying degrees of power in particular organizational structures in order to accomplish its stated goals. The political structures of the church include all of the patterns of relationships and decision making through which the community translates its faith into policy and action.

Politics pervades every aspect of the church's life. Worship, for instance, is never purely spontaneous. The church must plan its worship. Worship must happen at some time, in some place, and according to some form or order. Thus, a worship committee is formed, called to meet, and led by a chairperson to discuss the practical issues of when, where, and how the community will worship. The committee may be composed of five members and the minister, two of whom prefer a traditional worship pattern, one of whom prefers a contemporary order, and three of whom do not care. Points of view will be shared and argued, until finally one point of view emerges, a vote is taken, and a decision is made. Then the process begins all over again as the committee considers how best to present its decision to the governing body of the church. They discuss the attitudes they are likely to encounter, the arguments that may be set against their position, and the chances for passage. Someone is designated to speak on this or that point, and others are asked to be prepared to respond if the debate appears to be stalled. Thus, even the worship life of the church is highly politicized. The same is true of every aspect of the church's life. To deny the reality of politics in the church is to deny the very means by which the church as a human community lives.

Political processes in the church, as in other forms of human association, be they trade unions, state agencies, or business corporations, may be formal or informal. As a rule, trust and love are best served when political activity occurs within the polity. Political maneuvering within the context of a duly appointed worship committee, to return to our previous example, is relatively open to view. The meetings of the committee are announced. The agenda is public knowledge. The membership knows that the meetings of the committee are open and not secret. No one is threatened by the thought that things are happening in an unauthorized or illegitimate manner. One may not agree with the decision that is finally made, but one who has understood and acquiesced to the polity in advance will be more likely to accept an unpopular decision in trust and love when it has been made in the context of accepted procedure.

Informal political processes, however, always exist alongside the formal processes, and to deny them is unrealistic. A dinner party at which members of the church gather may become a political occasion. The business of the church may be discussed and opinions may be shared and shaped. Sometimes informal political processes facilitate the formal processes by cementing trust and love in informal personal contacts outside the formal meeting room. Sometimes informal political activity serves to confront the formal process with the minority point of view and, through suasion, to alter the position of the majority. In periods of great controversy in church and society, for example, informal groups that represent particular points of view often form for the purpose of influencing the policy and actions of the formal system. There is nothing morally wrong with these informal processes if the tactics employed are consistent with the institution's reason for being, but they do carry with them the danger of undercutting a fellowship based on trust and love.

Formal political processes are checked and balanced by constitutions, bylaws, organizational charts, and job descriptions, to which the membership has subscribed in advance. They are predictable and generally trusted by the membership. The informal political processes are less well defined, though equally real, constituted not by documents but by personal relationships and the exercise of effective personal influence. Thus, informal political processes are less predictable and more spontaneous. They tend to be distrusted. They often communicate disdain for the system rather than love. This does not have to be the case, of course, and sometimes it is not the case. At times, informal political activity has influenced the formal processes of the church in ways that have strengthened trust and love. Informal political activity is necessary to the church, especially when the bureaucracy has become cumbersome or out of touch either with the faith of the church or with the will of the membership. But there is always a healthy tension between the formal and informal political processes in the church when both are used responsibly. The task of leadership is twofold. It must keep the formal political processes open to the concerns being raised outside the system and especially to dissent from current policy and action. It must also keep the informal processes in a responsible relationship to the constituency as a whole.

Politics is the means by which the mission of the church is discerned and done in the formal and informal processes of its institutional life. It is the context in which the question of authority is answered in a voluntary association. It is the process by which values and goals are established, in which individuals are entrusted with leadership offices, and through which authority is granted or rescinded. All political activity in the church, be it formal or informal in nature, must be informed and judged by the church's historical understanding of its nature and mission as the people of God. The politics of the church are those patterns of human association that enable the church to reflect on and to participate in the politics of God, that is, in God's renovating activity in the world.

THE MINISTER AS A POLITICIAN

We do not often think of the minister as a politician. We think of the minister as a preacher of the Word, as a teacher of the faith, as a pastor of the people, as an administrator of an institution, and as a professional in the community at large. We often compare the Christian ministry to other professions, such as law or medicine, but seldom do we compare the minister to a politician. The social situation of a minister, however, is very different from that of a lawyer or a doctor. It is different in that a minister, unlike a lawyer or a doctor, must develop, nurture, and lead her own constituency. When the work of the minister is viewed from above, it is seen in a different light. The minister's constituency is the people of God, those whom God has called out into a worshiping, serving community of faith. From this point of view, God creates the minister's constituency as God works to renovate the fallen world.

Viewed from below as a social situation, however, the minister has no constituency apart from the constituency he builds. A judicatory may call a minister and place him in a field of work, but unless the minister creates a constituency by employing his knowledge, personal presence, and powers of suasion, a church will not likely be gathered. This is not true of a lawyer or a doctor. The lawyer is provided a constituency by the social situation itself. People live under the law. When legal advice is needed, they seek out a lawyer as the social instrument they need for that purpose. Likewise, the doctor is provided a constituency by the very nature of life itself. A person gets sick, needs medical attention, and goes to the physician for help. Lawyers and doctors work hard and do not succeed apart from their competence to do the task. But their constituencies are provided by the social complex in which all people live. Lawyers and doctors do not have to create the occasions for the delivery of their services. People need their services in order to survive happily and healthily in the world.

There may have been a time when the minister's constituency was provided by the social situation. The accepted attitudes of Western society, and especially of American society, once stacked the deck in favor of the church. Religion was highly respected as a mark of good character. Respectable people could be expected to participate in some form of organized religion. Applicants for scholarships, school admissions, and secular jobs often were asked about their religious preference and were judged harshly if they had none. Political candidates were judged as to their viability for office on the basis of their religious affiliation. There was a general sense of the promise of heaven and the threat of hell, and the church was considered to be the prime dispenser of grace and judgment.

Richard Baxter, author of the classic book *The Reformed Pastor* (1656), exclaimed to a minister who had inquired about the ministerial task, "Look upon your congregation believingly and with compassion. O speak not one cold or careless word about so great a business as heaven and hell."[27] Baxter understood the ministry essentially as a pastoral office, likening the minister to a shepherd and the people to a flock of sheep. There is much value still to be found in this seventeenth-century understanding of the task of the Reformed minister, but the world in which the minister lives today is radically different from Baxter's world. The church of Baxter's day was in the early stages of transition from a state church to a voluntary association. Most of the social and theological pressures of his day that still stacked the deck in favor of the church no longer exist today. The minister has a political task to perform today that Richard Baxter could scarcely have understood.

The contemporary minister lives and works within a free, pluralistic, secular, mobile, industrial, urban society, in which people decide to join or not to join a church with little or no social, economic, or political consequence. The minister, like the politician, must not only tend a constituency as a shepherd of sheep. The minister must develop that constituency by making those personal contacts, by acquiring those means of access to people, and by evoking that sense of loyalty both to the person and the convictions of the minister, to enable her to exert influence, to lead, and to pastor the people. The minister must be careful, of course, not to become the sole or primary center of loyalty. The minister's calling is to direct the loyalty of people to Jesus Christ. But there is no denying the fact that personal loyalty to the minister as the bearer of the church's faith in Christ is a part of a people's loyalty to Christ. Ministers need not be embarrassed by the affection of their people. This affection must never be the end of ministry, but the minister, like the politician, is the representative and bearer of the Christian claim. In order to function as such, the minister seeks a level of intimacy with people that naturally creates intimate personal ties, thereby facilitating the proclamation and reception of the gospel. The challenge of the ministry is to use the affection of a congregation for the glory of God rather than for the glory of the minister. "Whatever form this relationship takes," writes James Gustafson, "it is grounded in the social necessity of voluntary religious affiliation and institutions in our society—whether the voluntarism be theologically defended, juridically defended, or regarded as only an historical accident."[28]

In 1969 a book appeared, entitled *The Gathering Storm in the Churches*, which sought to reflect on the condition of the church as a human community in the light of the increased politicization of the institution over contemporary social and political issues.[29] This book had particular relevance for the time in which it was written, for the American religious community was becoming increasingly involved in the antiwar movement and other social issues. The insights of this book, however, continue to be instructive for one who seeks to understand the state of American Protestantism today. The situation today has not been radically altered since the book was written. The institutional church is still an institution in crisis, and no fair assessment can be made of the ministerial task apart from that crisis.

The central thesis set forth by the author, Jeffrey Hadden, grew out of numerous studies of American churches and church people. American Protestant churches, he reported, are involved in a deep and entangling crisis that threatens to disrupt or even to alter the nature of the church itself. The civil rights movement was the catalyst that unleashed the various elements of the contemporary crisis of American churches, but the sources of conflict have been latent in voluntary Protestant communities all along. Hadden identifies three ingredients of this crisis: the crisis of meaning and purpose, the crisis of belief, and the crisis of authority. The crisis of meaning and purpose refers to the absence of a consensus in the church about what the church is and ought to do. Some think that the church is a context of comfort and others that it is a context of challenge. The crisis of belief refers to the existence of doubt and uncertainty on the part of church people over what the Christian faith is and means. Many Christians today are not so much concerned about correct forms of worship or right forms of church government as they are about whether or not there is a God at all, or about whether Jesus was the revelation of God or just another good man. The crisis of authority, as we have already noted, refers to the absence of any clear norm or criterion with reference to which the mission and faith of the church may be clarified and molded into a Christian consensus. In an institution in which the meaning and purpose of the organization, the faith and values on which it is based, and the power to lead are questioned and obscured, the leadership task will likely be a profoundly political affair.

To characterize the ministerial task as political is to say four fundamental things about the work of the Christian minister. First, the minister, like the politician, is accountable to a constituency. The minister is accountable in two directions at once: theologically to the faith of the church and pastorally to the people of the church. This can be a difficult situation. On the one hand, the Reformed minister is accountable theologically to the gospel of Jesus Christ and to the Reformed tradition, in the context of which the minister understands what the gospel is and means. If the minister distorts the gospel or forsakes the historical tradition in and for which she was ordained, the minister risks making a ship-wreck of conscience. On the other hand, no minister is accountable to the gospel and a tradition alone, unless he is operating out of an independent organization over which he exercises control. The minister must gain the support of the major-ity of a congregation in order to be called as a minister of the church. Further-more, the minister must nurture a congregation in order to maintain sufficient support to continue to function as its spiritual leader. One of the tasks of lead-ership is to see that the institution provides its membership with sufficient rewards to assure their continued participation and support. If the minister rede-fines the meaning and purpose of the church, or alters the accustomed interpre-tation of the gospel, the membership must be persuaded to accept the validity of this reinterpretation, or else the minister must find a group of people with whom to work who agree with the new stance. Failure in this nurturing ministry will result in the demise of the group or in the loss of the minister's job. Gustafson uses this analogy:

> The pattern is more comparable to that of a congressman from a con-servative district who is interested in progressive reforms than it is to the local attorney or the physician. To stay in office, and yet to be more than the mirrored reflection of those who put and keep one in office, is close to the essence of a political process.[30]

Second, to say that the ministerial task is a political task is to say that the min-ister must be an effective communicator or teacher. This does not necessarily mean that the minister must be a classroom teacher, although the Reformed min-ister, ordained in a tradition that emphasizes education, gives up such opportu-nities at great peril. To say that a minister must be an effective communicator or teacher is to say that the minister's task, politically conceived, is one of shaping the mind of the constituency in the light of the gospel of Jesus Christ. The effec-tiveness of a minister will be determined largely by how successful the person is as a communicator of the Christian faith, that is, by the person's ability to direct and to redirect the thought, the convictions, the values, and the social perspec-tives of those to whom he or she is accountable. The task of the minister is to bring the claims of the church to bear upon the personal and social issues people face, by interpreting the faith of the church in the light of contemporary cir-cumstances, and by assisting people to live in the light of this faith in their per-sonal, social, and political existence.

Third, the minister as a politician must have a sense of vocation that tran-scends mere professionalism and gives to the ministry the identity of a sacred call-ing. The politician desires to be all things to all people, but no politician is able to do so without some overall perspective on who he or she is as a politician. The politician needs some transcending, integrating perspective on himself or herself as a person and on the office held, whether it be as a governor or a senator, and on what obligations and opportunities the office provides. Likewise, the minister must have some controlling sense of vocation that provides a sense of status or place in the whole scheme of things, a sense of belonging to an enterprise that transcends the immediate problems and goals of the particular institution. One does not have to look very far to see ministers with no vocational sense of who they are, or why they are who they are, or what they are called and ordained to do. For this reason, some ministers look to other disciplines, to business or to psychology or to government, for models and mentors that might assist them to know who they are as Christian ministers.

What gives the Reformed minister this sense of identity? Several things emerge out of the distinctive affirmations of Reformed faith to give the minister a sense of identity. One is the minister's own personal faith and devotion, for which there is no substitute. It is hard to be a minister without believing in God, trusting the forgiveness of sins, reading the Bible in personal devotion, and depending on the power of prayer. A ministry apart from deep personal commitment on the part of the minister to the God who is revealed in Jesus Christ and from the regular worship of God is doomed to failure. The Reformed tradition has always sought genuine piety in and from its ministers.

Another ingredient of ministerial identity is systematic study of the Bible and theology. Ministers who do their homework each week in the study, in sermon preparation but also above and beyond sermon preparation, are those who know and are given their sense of place by the substance of the faith itself. The pastor who cherishes pastoral identity as that of a theologian, and who persists in dialogue with the tradition of Christian believing, will not likely be troubled by the image issue or have difficulty with the question of who or what a minister is.

A third identifying characteristic is a certain holy arrogance. The Reformed minister not only passively believes the gospel but acts on the assumption that he has been called by Almighty God to the Christian ministry. A sense of identity that enables people to lead others does not come from nondirectiveness, nor does it issue in an apologetic or timid attitude concerning the ministerial office. Arrogance must be tempered by humility, with the minister always conscious of her sin and need for forgiveness, but humility is given its spine from the conviction of the call. The minister who trusts and believes the gospel, who applies time and energy to the source materials of the church's faith, and who functions vocationally on the assumption that God has called her to proclaim the gospel of Christ will be given whatever sense of identity is needed for the leading of the people.

Finally, the ministry requires considerable courage. There are times when the minister, like the politician, runs into trouble. There are times when the minister cannot develop a consensus within his constituency, when conscience calls the minister to stand over against the membership of the church, and when the minister must run the risk of losing a grip on the job. This does not happen often and, if it does, a minister will do well to ask why. The reason may be that positive leadership has not been given to the people in preaching, teaching, pastoral care, and administration, thereby withholding from them the categories of thought and experience that might have enabled them to respond as an enthusiastic, supportive constituency. But crises do come for the minister when everything must be risked for the sake of conviction. On these occasions, the minister experiences a vocational liability similar to that of a secular politician caught between conscience and the retention of the job.

To say that a minister is a politician is to admit that a minister has a somewhat different role within the church as a voluntary association than a lawyer or doctor within the society at large. The minister, like the politician, must develop, nurture, and maintain a constituency. The minister is accountable both to the gospel and to the church. The minister functions as a communicator and pastor of a people whom he is trying to shape and nurture. The minister requires a sense of office in order to lead, and sometimes must risk everything for the sake of conviction. The voluntary religious system has made politicians of all ministers. This is in no sense a negative assessment of the ministerial task. Rather, if God is in any sense a politician and uses the politics of the church in order to accomplish God's will and work, the political task of the minister is a high and holy calling. It is the constituency-building, association-nurturing task of a minister who is called to participate in God's renovating activity in the world.

THE EMERGENCE
OF THE CHURCH EXECUTIVE

Until very recently, the constitutions of most Protestant denominations made no provision for church executives: executive secretaries, executive presbyters, executive staffs, communicators, facilitators, coordinators, and others. The emergence of the church executive is a new phenomenon in Reformed communities, one that creates new problems as well as new possibilities for effective ministry. Our Reformed forebears, who gave considerable thought to church polity, envisioned no need for such positions. They could not have conceived of the church as we now know it—as a large institution, a multinational corporation, requiring executives and executive staff, extensive office facilities, and large budgets at the regional, national, and international levels. In those cases in which the organization had grown or developed beyond congregational proportions, policy was made and tasks were accomplished by volunteers or by ministers who interpreted these tasks as a part of their overall responsibility. With the growth of the church into large denominations and with the increasing centralization of power— as work that once was done on a local level was undertaken at a regional or national level and as new work was initiated—a new order of administrative functions and personnel was required. Orphanages and homes for elderly people were built and had to be overseen. Publishing houses, camps and retreat centers, schools and campus ministries, audio-visual departments, and fund-raising components were set in place and required employed staff. If Episcopal churches find their bishops functioning more like chief executive officers of American business corporations than ministers of the gospel, Presbyterian churches, which historically have resisted a government by bishops, find themselves increasingly living under an elaborate episcopacy of administrative personnel not originally envisaged by the polity. Executive officers of church judicatories often function as bishops, "not in the sense of elevated spiritual authorities, but in the sense of administrators of churches in a given area."[31]

Two additional factors have fostered the emergence of the church executive. One is the specialization of the ministry, whereby certain people have equipped themselves to serve the church in limited areas, such as Christian education, urban work, counseling, campus ministry, youth work, new church development, world hunger, and peace. Increasingly, the church relies on experts in highly complex fields of ministry to advise boards and agencies concerning their work. The other factor that has contributed to the rise of the church executive is the widening gap between the decision-making processes and the decision-enacting processes of the church. A church judicatory, for instance, may meet only once a year. In its meeting, it makes general and sometimes uninformed decisions concerning policy and action that have immediate and far-reaching implications for the life and work of the church. In order to enact these decisions, personnel must be employed, office space secured, and money allocated. Thus, denominational staff members live from day to day with little constitutional provision for accountability to the constituency at large, and wield great power between the meetings of the judicatories they serve. Sometimes, instead of simply enacting policy, they make policy, drawing their own inferences for program from the broad and general directives adopted by an annual meeting of a judicatory or committee. In many Protestant denominations, a power vacuum has been created by the growth and development of the church into a large, bureaucratic, established institution. From this power vacuum, the church executive has emerged as a significant political force in the life of the church.

The emergence of the church executive is not necessarily a bad thing. It may evidence the fact that the church as a human community is flexible and responsive enough to the contemporary requirements of the Christian community to reform itself into new patterns of leadership. Yet, there are dangers attendant upon the new office of church executive of which the church needs to be aware. The greatest danger of them all is that this new cadre of church administrators, living and working essentially outside the parameters of the polity, will become out of touch with the constituency they seek to serve and will live in a world all their own. The danger is that people exercising church power will lose their perspective on the mission, needs, desires, and expectations of the whole church by creating their own language, conversing essentially with themselves in their respective "shops," and acting with all good intentions contrary to the expectations of the membership. We have previously noted that the Reformed minister, functioning as a politician, lives in constant tension between the demands of the gospel and the expectations and needs of a constituency. This tension is less acute for the church executive than it is for the minister of a congregation, if only because the constituency is geographically dispersed and remote from the executive's office. The result is that the demands of the gospel and the expectations and needs of the constituency may become subordinated to administrative processes and budget directives. Reformed churches in the United States, like other Protestant bodies, have yet to come to terms with the place of the church executive in their theology of ordination and Christian vocation and in their systems of church government. This represents a major challenge to the integrity of the polity and politics of these churches for the future.

Chapter 8

The Ministry of the Church

The Christian Church is the congregation of the brethren in which Jesus Christ acts presently as the Lord in Word and sacrament through the Holy Spirit. As the Church of pardoned sinners, it has to testify in the midst of a sinful world, with its faith as with its obedience, with its message as with its order, that it is solely his property, and that it lives and wants to live solely from his comfort and from his direction in the expectation of his appearance.

We reject the false doctrine, as though the Church were permitted to abandon the form of its message and order to its own pleasure or to changes in prevailing ideological and political convictions.

The Theological Declaration of Barmen

The ministry of the church is always a subject for lively discussion and debate whenever Christian people pause to reflect on the meaning and purpose of their life together. To some people, the church is a source of comfort and help in a troubled world; to others, the church is an agent of social change that should challenge people to confront injustice in society. For some, the ministry of the church should concern itself primarily with the individual's relationship to Jesus Christ, providing a warm and supportive context for the birth and maturation of personal faith. For others, the ministry of the church is primarily a ministry of outreach to people with spiritual or physical needs outside of the believing fellowship. In recent years, churches have seized upon various management tactics, involving information gathering, evaluation, prioritizing, and goal setting, in an effort to discern what the church is to be and to do. Some of these procedures may have been edifying for the church, if only because they have enabled the laity to gain a better grasp on the presuppositions and intentions of its leaders. For the most part, however, these processes have resulted in few revelations. The ministry of the church is not something the church locates through process. The ministry of the church is given of Christ, and though the forms that it takes change from time to time, the ministry itself remains constant.

CHARACTERISTICS OF THE MINISTRY OF THE CHURCH

The ministry of the church is definite, limited, and full of promise.[1] It is definite in that it is given and defined by the revelation of God in the life, death, resurrection, and expected coming of Jesus Christ. The Confession of 1967 of the Presbyterian Church (U.S.A.) defines the ministry or mission of the church as follows:

> The life, death, resurrection, and promised coming of Jesus Christ has set the pattern for the church's mission. His life as a man involves the church in the common life of men. His service to men commits the church to work for every form of human well-being. His suffering makes the church sensitive to all the sufferings of mankind so that it sees the face of Christ in the faces of men in every kind of need. His crucifixion discloses to the church God's judgment on man's inhumanity to man and the awful consequences to its own complicity in injustice. In the power of the risen Christ and the hope of his coming the church sees the promise of God's renewal of man's life in society and of God's victory over all wrong.
>
> The church follows this pattern in the form of its life and in the method of its action. So to live and serve is to confess Christ as Lord.[2]

That is to say, the world does not set the agenda for the church. The church is influenced by the world, by the needs and problems of contemporary people, and by the issues that are raised in contemporary society, but the ministry of the church is a given. It is to bear witness to Jesus Christ and to God's renovating activity revealed and demonstrated in him. W. A. Visser 't Hooft, a twentieth-century Dutch Reformed theologian, said that the ministry of the church is to be the church, to bear witness to Jesus Christ, to testify to the world that the church exists, and thus to serve the purposes of God.[3]

The church is always tempted to forget that it exists solely for the purpose of bearing witness to Jesus Christ. It is easy for a congregation to become a social club or a welfare organization. Denominational bureaucracies tend to develop a life of their own in the context of which people sometimes forget or deny that the structure exists for the ministry and serves no other useful purpose. We have already noted that the church is a human community and functions like other communities. But the church as a human community always lives with reference to its ministry, which is its norm. The church may do many useful things in society, but if it does not bear witness to Jesus Christ, it is not the church. The ministry of the church, therefore, is limited by definition. It is limited by the fact that it is ministry. It is not neutral, passive coexistence with God. It is not a mandate to dominate or control. The ministry of the church is active service to God and people in subordination to Jesus Christ. It is a ministry to God in which people are served, and a ministry to people in which God is served. The most graphic image in this regard is the biblical image of the servant of God, who serves God by bringing his forgiveness to people and serves people by bearing their guilt before God. Jesus Christ was the perfect servant of God. "Now the community ministers, however imperfectly, in His school and discipleship."[4] But the church has no power to guarantee the results of its work. To say that the task of the church is ministry is to admit that the church is no more and no less than a servant of the reconciling, restoring grace of God, and that the outcome or results of its service must be left in God's hands.

The ministry of the church is also limited by the fact that it is a ministry of witness bearing, not of institutional self-promotion. The task of the church is to point beyond itself to Jesus Christ as the light of the world. The church itself is not the light of the world, nor is the church called to analyze, criticize, and explain the darkness. The ministry of the church is to attest to the presence of Jesus Christ in the darkness, standing over against the world in testifying to what it knows, yet standing with the world as a recipient of God's judgment and grace. As a witness bearer, the church is not called to effect that which it proclaims—God's unparalleled renovation of the world. It is called to do no less, and no more, than to bear witness to what God has done and is doing to renew creation, according to the faith and knowledge that has been granted to it.

Finally, the church undertakes its ministry confident that it is full of promise. It does so in the assurance that "its cause is righteous, that as it discharges it according to the measure of its knowledge and resources it is not left to its own knowledge and resources, and that it does not finally act in vain."[5] The promise under which the church lives is none other than the gospel in and by which it is constituted and called to ministry as the church. It is the sustaining power of the Word of God, the reality of the forgiveness of sins, the foretaste of the new life in Christ, and the living hope that transcends defeat and death that assures the church that its labor is not in vain. The promise is never possessed by the church as an object, nor is it ever absolutely clear that the promise is true, for the promise is always a gift of God received in faith. Yet the church is never without authenticating signs of the promise, such as fresh courage to undertake some difficult task, personal or financial resources for ministry that are neither merited nor anticipated, and a clear sense of God's presence and guidance in the midst of a decision-making process. The church lives not by its achievements but only by these signs of promise, which give to it the needed assurance that its ministry is and will be fulfilled in Jesus Christ.

THE THREEFOLD NATURE
OF THE CHURCH'S MINISTRY

The ministry of the church to bear witness to Jesus Christ takes place in the proclamation, the explication, and the application of the gospel with which the church is entrusted. These are not identical tasks, but they are so interdependent that each is implicit and explicit in the other.

First, the ministry of the church is to proclaim the gospel. Whatever may be said about the ministry of the church, whatever else the church may plan, attempt, or accomplish, its ministry is essentially to proclaim the faith that the God who created the heavens and the earth is revealed in certain normative events in the history of Israel, and supremely in Jesus Christ, as the God of mercy and of grace. It is to declare God as the living God, the reality with reference to whom all other realities are more or less significant, the one with whom people daily have to do. It is to announce that God encounters people because he loves them, forgives their sins, reconciles people to God, unites them one with another, and gives direction to their lives. The ministry of the church is to proclaim the gospel of God, introducing its claims into the realm of human discourse and decision, and testifying thereby that a people exists who believe that the gospel is true. In the church's proclamation or representation, the gospel lives in contemporary history as a historical fact.

The church proclaims the gospel in many ways and in different forms: directly and indirectly, explicitly and implicitly, in spoken words or in profound silence, in conscious acts and premeditated deeds or in intentional abstention from acting and doing. The gospel may be proclaimed by the church as a community of the whole or by the church through its individual members. Whatever may be its way or form of proclamation, the ministry of the church is publicly to declare what God has done and is doing to renovate the fallen world. As it does so, the church must indicate what the gospel means and apply its truth to contemporary life, but neither the explication nor the application of the gospel can ever replace the simple declaration of its truth. There is a level of Christian apperception that cannot be explicated and applied from without but that must be apprehended within as one hears the simple announcement of grace ("In Jesus Christ, we are forgiven") and receives it by faith. When the ministry of proclamation is not exercised, the church ceases to be the church, and the good news of life is withheld from the world.

Second, the ministry of the church is to explicate the gospel, explaining what it means and showing how it makes itself intelligible to people. In one sense, it may be said that the gospel explicates itself. God wills to be known. God speaks in order to be understood. The Word became flesh that we might not only hear but behold God's glory. The God who wills to be known grants faith to the beholder and gives to faith its true understanding and knowledge. Hence, it may be said that God both proclaims and explicates the gospel to the human heart, and that all human proclamation and explication is but the faithful following of the course previously charted by Another.

In another sense, however, the gospel both lends itself to the processes of reason and requires the exercise of reason for its contemporary understanding and appropriation. Human beings are intelligent beings, for whom intelligibility is crucial to commitment. "What cannot be thought through critically and expressed with reasonable clarity," states John Leith, "cannot demand the allegiance of man's whole being."[6] Furthermore, the language and thought forms by which the gospel is transmitted from one generation to another are radically historical. That is to say, they are intimately related to the time, events, language, and culture of the historical period in which they gain currency, and often lose their power to communicate in succeeding generations. Therefore, the gospel must be in dialogue with the vehicles by which it is communicated in every generation; faith must always search for more adequate means of understanding. The ministry of explication consists of a narration of the normative events and convictions of the past, a clarification of these things in the light of the contemporary situation, and a clarification of the contemporary situation in the light of these things. The whole of church history may be viewed as a constant attempt on the part of the Christian community not only to proclaim the gospel to the world but to clarify its content, to explain its meaning, and to render it intelligible.

Third, the ministry of the church is the application of the gospel. The church does not proclaim and explicate the gospel in a vacuum, just as it does not live in a vacuum but in relation to the particular human realities, needs, questions, problems, and possibilities of the world in which it lives. This ministry rests upon the conviction that God is a living God, whose love for people is particular and contemporary and whose will is to encounter people "where they really are what they are and where they may be reached when addressed."[7] The presupposition is that God has made and loves contemporary men and women, that Jesus died and rose again for them as well as for people of old, and that faith in God and obedience to God's will are the first and final destiny of people today as well as yesterday. The church has no other option than to love those whom God loves, to proclaim and to explicate the gospel in love to those loved by God. The ministry of application is the evangelical appeal, whereby the gospel is presented to contemporary people in such a way that they come to see its application to them and are summoned to a life of faith and service.

In order to fulfill this ministry, the church must know people as well as love them, acquaint itself with the culture by which they are nurtured, concern itself with the existential issues they face, and equip itself to deal constructively with the challenge of other systems or philosophies of life. This is the church's warrant for interdisciplinary conversation and research. The church must be willing to leave its protected position, granted it either by common consent or cultural indifference, and commerce in the realm of conflicting ideas, engaging people not as heathens, atheists, unbelievers, or whatever, but as those whom God has reconciled and called. The church fulfills its ministry when it demonstrates the gospel in such a way as to move people to faith and draw them into the circle of the kingdom of God. The ministry of application, as well as that of proclamation and explication, is fulfilled only when the church undertakes it with great humility, conscious of the fact that it shares with the world in an absolute equality of need, and mindful of the fact that although it is privileged to proclaim the one who comes to judge and redeem the earth, the church is not worthy to stoop down and untie his sandals (Mark 1:7).

THE FORMS OF THE CHURCH'S MINISTRY

The threefold ministry of the church is undertaken and fulfilled in various forms or vocations. Some forms of the church's ministry are primarily forms of speech by which the church bears verbal witness to Jesus Christ. Other forms of the church's ministry are primarily forms of action whereby the church demonstrates its faith in the gospel. In all forms, however, speech and action cannot be far removed from one another. Speaking is action, and actions often speak louder than words. On the other hand, actions need words of interpretation if people are to be apprehended by the gospel there proclaimed, explicated, and applied; and speech must be incarnate in life if it is to bear witness to the incarnation of God in Jesus Christ. Regardless of how we distinguish between the various forms or functions of the church's ministry, each represents a particular way of combining speech and action in witness to Jesus Christ. Although one form of ministry may emphasize speech and the other may emphasize action, no form of the church's ministry represents the one without the other.

Karl Barth has conveniently, if arbitrarily, organized the various forms of the church's ministry into twelve categories, consisting of six forms of ministry in which speech is predominant (praise, preaching, teaching, evangelism, missions, and theology) and six forms of ministry in which action is predominant (prayer, the cure of souls, personal witness, service, prophetic action, and fellowship).[8] One may argue with the arrangement of the forms under these particular headings (e.g., evangelism today may be more faithfully done when action predominates over speech), but few will argue that these forms misrepresent the scope of the apostolic ministry of the church. In this chapter we will make use of Barth's analysis and seek to illustrate its contemporary relevance for the church.

The ministry of the church is the praise of God in Christian worship. To praise God in Christian worship is to affirm, acknowledge, and celebrate both the existence of God as revealed in Jesus Christ and the activity of God whereby God renovates the fallen world. When the church praises God in Christian worship, it puts its interior devotion and external commitments into liturgical forms of language and music, offering to God the service God is due, raising the church's banner of fealty as witness to the world, and anticipating what in the light of God's future consummation of all things will be the joyful response of the whole creation. Furthermore, the praise of God in Christian worship is the context in which faith is born and nurtured. In uttering its praise of God, the church acts in such a way as to proclaim, explicate, and apply the gospel to the lives of people.

> To see a person you know kneel in prayer is to have his testimony
> that God is, that God is available for guidance and strength, and that
> the believer recognizes the contingencies and limitations of his life in
> the total scheme of things.[9]

Reformed worship may be said to be Calvinistic in that John Calvin heavily influenced the worship of the Reformed community of the sixteenth century. As an active pastor in Strasbourg and Geneva, Calvin took worship seriously and worked out Reformed liturgies for his congregations that continue to influence the worship of Reformed churches today. In all of his harsh criticism of medieval Catholic worship, Calvin could not bring himself to say that the worship of the church was without any merit at all. He felt that God had preserved "traces of the Church" in medieval practice, such as the sacrament of Baptism, as vestiges of the truth.[10] However, he felt that the worship practices he had known from his youth were an "ill-patched hodgepodge," the pattern for which had been taken "from the ravings of the Gentiles" and "the ancient rites of Mosaic law, which apply to us no more than do animal sacrifices and other like things."[11] Calvin believed that most of the ceremonies and rites of the church benumbed people rather than proclaiming, explicating, and applying evangelical truth to their lives. Thus, he considered the reformation of worship to be one of his most important tasks, and he gave to it great thought and attention.

Other factors also contributed to the history and character of Reformed worship. Huldrich Zwingli (1484–1531), pastor of the Grossmünster in Zurich, and William Farel (1489–1565), who preceded Calvin in St. Peter's Church in Geneva, left their mark on Reformed worship. In Zurich, the Reformation was born and nourished in the context of Zwingli's systematic preaching of the Bible. For Zwingli, worship was primarily a preaching occasion; and nothing was permitted to distract from the proclamation, explication, and application of the gospel in the sermon. Farel was a "venturesome, big-voiced, red-bearded little evangelist and controversialist,"[12] who went to Geneva in 1533 and led that city to cast its lot with the Reformation. In 1534, the bishop's vicar, who was in charge of the city at the time, forbade the reading of the Bible. Farel preached in homes, in churches when permitted, and even from the ramparts of the city. On one dramatic occasion, he was carried by the crowd to St. Peter's Church, where on August 8, 1535, the first Protestant sermon was heard in that church. The place given to preaching in Reformed worship today reflects the influence of Zwingli and Farel.

Reformed worship was also influenced by the Puritan movement in England and America. The Puritans introduced Calvinism to the mind and practice of the Anglican Church. They opposed the use of prayer books because it contributed to a lazy ministry and obscured the significance of preaching in worship. Reformed worship was also influenced by the experience of Reformed communities in America.[13] When Reformed Christians arrived in the New World, they brought with them a variety of worship experience and attitudes. Some were accustomed to the worship of continental Reformed churches, some to that of the Church of Scotland, some to the forms of the Church of England, and some to the more radical practices of the Puritan tradition. Worship in America often took place not in a stately cathedral but in a schoolhouse or out of doors. The shortage of ministers necessitated increased lay responsibility for Christian worship and education, and congregations of various historical traditions often met together. Thus, the American experience added elements of tolerance, diversity, freedom, and informality to Reformed worship.

Reformed worship admits to considerable freedom and diversity in its forms and practices, but it is not without definite character. First, Reformed worship is focused upon the praise of God, not on the experience of the worshiper. Second, it testifies to the centrality and authority of the Bible in Christian faith and practice. Third, it emphasizes the importance of personal and corporate prayer. Fourth, it emphasizes the singing of the psalms and other hymns that depend heavily on the Bible for their content. Fifth, Reformed worship emphasizes the importance of preaching as a means of grace. Sixth, it reflects the importance of the sacraments of Baptism and the Lord's Supper in Christian faith and life. Reformed worship may be ordered in various ways, reflecting considerable freedom and diversity, but whenever Reformed people worship, one may expect these six characteristics to be implicitly or explicitly expressed.

The praise of God in Christian worship is the heart of the church's ministry. When the church assembles for worship, it is constantly reminded of who it is and of what it has been given to do, and it receives the insight and strength its ministry requires. The worship assembly, however, is also an act of witness whereby the church testifies to the fact that a people exists who believe the gospel to be true and are determined to order their lives accordingly. Finally, the praise of God is an enormously formative event in the development of Christian character. Human personality is shaped by worship. In worship a person's whole being is centered on and focused by an external reality and claim as in few other times in life. Therefore, the praise of God is one of the indispensable forms of the ministry of the church.

The ministry of the church is to preach the gospel. Mention has already been made of the importance of preaching in the Reformed tradition and of the influence of Zwingli, Farel, and the Puritans in this regard. John Calvin thought so highly of preaching that he felt it was "the means of grace above all others" by which God would transform the city of Geneva, and to this end he preached more than three thousand sermons.[14] The Protestant Reformation was one of the greatest revivals of preaching in the history of the Christian church.

"What is at issue in preaching?" Karl Barth asked rhetorically. "Decisively that the community, and with it the world, should remind itself or be reminded explicitly of the witness with which it is charged, that it should find reassurance as to its content, that reflected in it Jesus Christ Himself should speak afresh to it, that it should be summoned afresh to His service in the world."[15] Christian preaching is the preaching of Jesus Christ—the proclamation, explication, and application of what God has done and is doing in him to renovate the fallen world—and the call of the church to its ministry of witness.

True preaching is rooted and grounded in the biblical message as transmitted in the books of the Old and New Testaments. It presupposes thorough scholarship and the critical study of the Bible, as well as a faithful listening for God's Word on the part of the preacher in, with, and under the words of the text. The preaching of Jesus Christ rests on biblical studies and gains authenticity from the preacher's personal faith and commitment. But preaching is always more than a simple exposition of Scripture. Preaching is the proclamation of the gospel to which the Bible bears authoritative witness, but it is not the preaching of or about the Bible itself. In the words of the Theological Declaration of Barmen, "Jesus Christ, as he is attested for us in Holy Scripture, is the one Word of God which we have to hear and which we have to trust and obey in life and in death."[16] Hours of study and preparation lie behind the true preaching of Jesus Christ.

> Discussions of relations in Jerusalem at the time of the war between Syria and Ephraim, or of the nature and activities of the scribes, Pharisees and Sadducees at the time of Jesus, or of the errors and confusions of the community at Corinth, together with the relevant literary, historical and archaeological data, must certainly occupy the one who has to preach on the texts concerned, but they must be left on one side in the actual event of preaching.[17]

Preaching is neither a retelling of the text nor is it a display of the preacher's intellectual diligence to the details of exegesis. Preaching is the theological task of declaring what the gospel is, of exposing what the gospel means, and of addressing the gospel appeal to the lives of contemporary people. It seeks to enliven the point of intersection where the ancient biblical text, the history of Christian discourse, and the realities of particular people meet, critique one another, and render the gospel of God intelligible to contemporary life. It is a call to faith rather than unbelief, to obedience instead of disobedience, to knowledge instead of ignorance. It reminds the church of who it is and of what it is to do, invites people into its circle of meaning, and equips them for their ministry in the world.

Preaching is often disparaged in the contemporary church by those who either chafe under its discipline or become discouraged at its apparent inefficacy in the determination of human affairs. It is sometimes displaced by the introduction of more spectacular forms of liturgy, by a primary emphasis on the sacraments, by a preference for social action, or by the transformation of the preaching event into a dramatic performance on the part of the preacher. Yet there is no convincing evidence that language has lost its power to proclaim, explicate, and apply the gospel to the minds and hearts of contemporary people. The church disparages the ministry of preaching at its own peril. If the church in the Reformed tradition has at times overemphasized preaching and stands to gain from the recovery of other forms of catholic worship, its emphasis on the ministry of preaching nevertheless has issued in a pattern of Christian discipleship that honors some of the highest powers of human personality: the service of God in the life of the mind, the ability to think and act in freedom and independence, the critical capacity to discern reality from superstition, the ability to transcend and to criticize oneself and one's social involvements, and the facility to transform the culture in ways that more nearly reflect beliefs and values.[18] The efficacy of preaching in the determination of human affairs is difficult to measure. When the church preaches Jesus Christ, it refrains from all measurement in trust that God's Word shall not return to him empty, that God will accomplish that which God purposes, and that the church will prosper in the thing for which God sent it (Isa. 55:11).

The ministry of the church is teaching—the instruction of the church, and the instruction by the church of the world, in the knowledge of God. The church is more than a school, but along with other things, the church is also a school of faith in which men and women are educated for their ministry in the world.

The ministry of teaching and learning has long been cherished by Reformed people. The leaders of the Swiss Reformation were men who had been liberated by humanistic learning. The revival of Renaissance learning and scholarship, spread by means of books and personal associations, influenced a number of clergy and educated laypersons, and created a climate of criticism and ridicule toward traditional ecclesiasticism and theology. Zwingli, being influenced by Erasmus, the prince of humanists, received a classical humanist education in preparation for the priesthood, as did Oecolampadius, Bullinger, and others. John Calvin was a consummate humanist and scholar before he was a theologian and reformer. The humanist tradition of the sixteenth century, in which the life of the mind was honored and critical scholarship was cultivated, greatly influenced the whole future of the Reformed movement. Faith and learning were understood as complementary and reciprocal activities that are integral to the Christian life. Initially, the emphasis was on a learned ministry, an emphasis that persists in Reformed churches today. An academy was established in Geneva to educate prospective clergy. The Puritans carried this emphasis on an educated ministry to America, where in 1636 they founded Harvard College "to advance Learning and to perpetuate it to Posterity, dreading to leave an illiterate Ministry to the Churches when our present Ministers shall lie in the Dust."[19] Later, the concern for education was broadened to include the laity. The academy in Geneva soon became a university and Harvard College by no means limited itself to the education of ministers. Wherever Reformed people settled, schools were built as well as churches, not only that people might be educated in the Bible but in the liberal arts as well.

The ministry of teaching presupposes that, although there may be some exceptions, normally there is a need for certain basic information if a person is to hear and believe the gospel. One must be informed of certain events in the history of Israel and understand their meaning; one must know that a man named Jesus lived, died, and is believed to have risen from the dead. Beyond these basic facts, there is a wealth of interpretation and experience that is immensely helpful to one who is considering the validity ofy ofy of the Chr Chr Chre task of the church is to impart the information that is necessary for Christian faith and life to those within who seek to grow in faith, and to those outside the church who have yet to come to faith.

In the broadest sense, theology (*theos,* "god"; *logos,* "word" or "knowledge") is the study of our knowledge of God, the attempt to serve God with the mind. Theology involves thinking as rigorously and honestly as possible about who God is and what God intends for our lives. Anselm, an eleventh-century theologian, defined theology as faith in search of understanding. That is to say, believing in God is not enough. Faith must seek understanding if it is to grow and endure. Thus, theology is the calling of every Christian, not just of the specialist in the theological seminary. If theology means loving God with the mind, then every Christian is called to this task. If theology is faith in search of understanding, then no one can be exempted from the responsibility of understanding what he or she believes. The task of the church, therefore, is to teach people to be theologians, to help people to think theologically, and to instruct people in the knowledge of God, that they may love God with their minds as well as their hearts and wills.

Theology is incumbent upon every Christian for other reasons. First, each Christian is called to the theological task by the doctrine of the priesthood of all believers. In the Reformed understanding of the church, no individual, group, or theology is infallible, authoritative, or universally applicable. Theology is a process of Christian dialogue or discourse about God in the context of which individuals seek to discern truth from error in their engagement one with another. All persons and points of view need to be subject to question and challenge in the community of Christian discourse. In such interchange, we incarnate the priesthood of all believers. Second, Christians must be prepared give account for the hope that is in them (1 Pet. 3:15) or to defend the faith against challenge or attack from competing points of view. For this, some knowledge of the Bible, its possible interpretations, the history and thought of the church, and current theological developments are indispensable. According to Barth, "The statement: 'I am a mere layman and not a theologian,' is evidence not of humility but of indolence."[20] Third, the Christian must be in a position to analyze and not be bewildered by the dramas, tragedies, calamities, and progressions of personal, ecclesiastical, and societal life from a theological perspective. The Christian must be prepared to discern the signs of the times, to distinguish between the spirits of the age, and to make ethical decisions concerning highly complex matters. These things are not simply or easily done. The Christian must be taught if such witness is to be born to Jesus Christ. To that end, all Christians are and forever remain catechumens as long as they live. The ministry of the church is to catechize or instruct them in the knowledge of God.

The ministry of the church is evangelism, or that part of the task which was once called home missions. It is widely assumed that the Protestant Reformers had little concern for evangelism and missions. Paul D. L. Avis has tried to establish that the Reformers had more concern for these things than historians have acknowledged.[21] Nevertheless, one cannot deny that there is a strange silence in the writings of the Reformers on evangelism and missions. Until 1684, when the Peace of Westphalia brought the Thirty Years' War to an end, Protestants in Germany were fighting for their survival. Similar struggles in other lands sapped the energy of those whose primary concern was to reform the church. When they were not fighting Rome, they were often fighting one another. Furthermore, the world loomed large and the Reformers had few firsthand experiences with heathen peoples. One exception was the Anabaptist movement. The Anabaptists were evangelists rather than church reformers, who laid great stress on personal commitment and a decision for faith. If the magisterial Reformers assumed that personal evangelism and world missions had essentially been completed in the early Christian centuries, the Anabaptists sought to revive the apostolic mission to the unbeliever near and far. "Our faith stands on nothing other than the command of Christ," they said, "for Christ did not say to his disciples, 'Go forth and celebrate the mass,' but, 'Go forth and preach the gospel.'"[22]

In the present context, and for purposes of clarification, evangelism will be distinguished from world missions by limiting it to the evangelization of those who live culturally and geographically in the environs of the church but who do not share its faith, knowledge, or ministry. There is in Western culture an untended gate or shifting frontier between the church and the world. Where there is little or no separation of church and state, people become members of the church by virtue of their birth and citizenship, with minimal regard for personal decision or the act of commitment. Where church membership is voluntary, people join the church for a variety of reasons, to meet the right people or to improve social standing, for example, and are retained on church rolls even though they manifest little or no interest. Thus, the church includes in its membership thousands of people who neither know nor care to know what is at stake in being Christian. The gospel is as strange to them as it is to unbelievers who live in a foreign land.

The ministry of evangelism is the proclamation, explication, and application of the gospel to people who culturally and geographically live close to the church; who ought long since to have heard and believed the gospel, but in fact have not; who have either not joined the church or have fallen away from the church, or for whom church membership is meaningless. Karl Barth suggested that "evangelization serves to awaken this sleeping Church,"[23] but it does more than that. Evangelization seeks to activate the latent church, that is, those for whom Christ died, whom God has redeemed, but who have not yet become what they already are. The purpose of this evangelization is not to criticize or condemn those to whom the ministry is addressed. It is to declare to them that God's grace and love in Jesus Christ applies specifically to them, to proclaim to them that their salvation is assured, and to invite them to accept this reality and to share the ministry of the church.

The church lives today in a pluralistic, secular, technological, mobile, rootless, urban world. In this world, few legal, psychological, social, or theological pressures remain to compel people to be Christian and to join the church. The church is a more radically voluntary association than it has been since the first century, and people are more radically free to belong or not to belong than ever before. Consequently, whether in rebellion against old authorities or by simple preference, many people live apart from the church. Old traditions, memories, stories, and values that once gave definition to life and located people in a certain circle of meaning have been lost. Many people in this society, being now traditionless, are also lost and adrift. Some, for whom the vacuum is particularly threatening, will be victimized by alien movements and traditions that are personally and socially destructive. It has been rightly said that the secular, pluralistic world in which the church lives today is not an occasion for despair but an opportunity for a renewed interest in Christian evangelism.[24] The challenge before the church today is to proclaim, explicate, and apply its traditions and memories persuasively so that people who are lost will come to believe that the gospel is their life and the church their true home.

The ministry of the church is world missions. World missions is undertaken when the church reaches out beyond its own confession and culture to those who do not live in the environs of its message or ministry. World missions is the response of the church to the great commission given it by its Lord: "Go therefore and make disciples of all nations, baptizing them in the name of the Father and of the Son and of the Holy Spirit, and teaching them to obey everything that I have commanded you" (Matt. 28:19–20).

The Reformers, even when they commented on Matthew 28, did not exhort the church to world missions, but they were not bereft of the apostolic vision, nor were they totally uninvolved in missionary activity. In 1555, for instance, John Calvin was approached by Durand de Villegaignon about sending pastors from Geneva to minister to a small Huguenot community in Brazil. Two Genevan pastors were commissioned to go to Brazil, not only to minister to the Huguenot families residing there but also to convert the natives to Christianity.[25] In 1664, Justinian Ernest von Welz, a Lutheran, exhorted his fellow Lutherans to accept the challenge of world missions. About the same time, the Moravian community began to show interest in missions, as did the Puritans in their activity in North America. If the Reformers did not emphasize world missions adequately, at least it may be said that they revived the gospel and reformed the church, thus setting the stage for the later growth of missionary activity.

The modern mission movement has its roots in the work of William Carey, a Baptist minister and a cobbler who published an "Enquiry into the Obligation of Christians to Use Means for the Conversion of the Heathens." As a result of Carey's zeal for world missions, the Baptist Society for Propagating the Gospel Among the Heathen was begun in 1792. The nineteenth century, however, was the great missionary century in the history of the church, and Reformed church people played a leading role in its growth and development. Great changes in the theology and practice of world missions took place in the twentieth century in response to the growing self-consciousness of the so-called younger churches, as well as to the politicization of those societies often referred to collectively as the "third world." The World Missionary Conference that met in Edinburgh in 1910 set the stage for an ecumenical missionary theology and practice and thus is regarded as an epoch-making event in modern mission history. Among other things, the Edinburgh conference brought to the fore such men as D. S. Cairns and John MacMurray of Scotland, A. G. Hogg of India, William Temple of England, and John R. Mott and Robert E. Speer of the United States, who would be the leaders of the missionary movement in the years to come. The conclusions of this conference may be summarized in five propositions. First, Christianity, by which was meant the essential revelation rather than the body of belief and practice, is absolute. "Jesus Christ fulfills and supersedes all other religions" (Report of the Commission on the Christian Message). Second, Christians must seek out the nobler elements in non-Christian religions and use them as steps to higher things. Third, all religions disclose the needs of the soul, which Jesus alone can satisfy. Fourth, the higher forms of non-Christian religions manifest the working of the Holy Spirit. Fifth, Christianity, understood here as faith and practice, is enriched by insights from other religions.

A quarter of a century later, the second great World Missionary Conference was held in Jerusalem. The dominating fact at this meeting was the rise of secularism. The central question here concerned the relative importance of the spiritual values inherent in non-Christian religions. For the first time, secularism was considered to be one of the religions of the world with which the Christian missionary enterprise had to come to terms. The conference recognized as part of the one truth the sense of the majesty of God and the consequent reverence found in Islam; the deep sympathy for the world's sorrow and the unselfish search for a way of escape found in Buddhism; the desire for contact with ultimate reality conceived as spiritual that is prominent in Hinduism; the belief in a moral order of the universe and the consequent insistence on moral conduct in Confucianism; and the disinterested pursuit of truth and of human welfare found in those who stand for secular civilization but do not accept Jesus Christ as their Lord and Savior.

The third World Missionary Conference was held in Tambaran, India, in 1938, in preparation for which Hendrik Kraemer wrote the volume, *The Christian Message in a Non-Christian World*, that was to dominate both the conference and mission discussion for decades thereafter. Kraemer sought to distinguish Christianity as a religion from the revelation of God in Jesus Christ, asserting that Christianity is one religion among others, while Jesus Christ is absolutely "sui generis" (i.e., in a category all his own). Furthermore, he drew a sharp distinction between God's revelation in Jesus Christ and all religious experience, suggesting that one could have an authentic experience of God, such as that known to the Jews, and still reject Jesus Christ. The conference debated such questions as whether or not there is a genuine self-disclosure of God in non-Christian religious experience and, if so, how the uniqueness of Jesus Christ could be maintained. The questions raised by Kraemer and debated at Tambaran precipitated a tragic break in the dialogue between Christian and non-Christian religions. The assertion of discontinuity between the revelation of God in Jesus Christ and all religion undercut the sense of common ground that had previously been assumed to be the basis of dialogue by representatives of the various religions.

Although dialogue between the great religions of the world has been revived since Tambaran, the emphasis of the conversation is not the same as before. Today the question is not centered on the issue of the finality of Jesus Christ or of the relation of Christianity to non-Christian religious experience but on the place of Christ in secular history. The universal process of secularization has channeled the debate in other directions, especially in the third world nations, where poor and oppressed peoples seek social and political alternatives to their old colonial dependencies. Today all religious traditions are being challenged to evidence resources that are relevant to the revolutionary situation existing in third world countries.[26] There is a strong conviction in these countries that God is at work in the revolutionary social change of the time, liberating oppressed peoples from bondage. The Bible is being read by third world peoples as the story of God's liberating activity in the world, which provides clues as to how and where God is operative in the world today. The church in its missionary activity is considered to be irrelevant both to the gospel and to the world it is called to serve when it chooses to be inactive in the quest for social, political, and economic justice.

The church must proclaim, explicate, and apply the gospel to particular people in terms of the concrete personal, social, political, and economic realities of their lives. To be insensitive to the historical context in which people live and hear the gospel is to deny its power to confront and transform the real world. The present danger to the missionary enterprise of the church, however, is not insensitivity to the material circumstances of oppressed peoples but insensitivity to the cries for meaning that finally question whether or not historical existence is worth living at all. In the midst of all social, political, and economic movements and systems, children are born, people are afflicted by illness, tragedy interrupts well-laid plans, and the strong as well as the weak face death. The crucial issue before the church today concerns the church's continuing trust, or lack of it, that the gospel with which it has been entrusted is true, that it is the transforming, sustaining reality applicable to all people. If it is so, then the church still has a story to tell to the nations.

In a world that seems capricious if not malevolent, the gospel offers a sense of meaning, claiming that love and creativity are clues to an understanding of that world. In a world that is characterized by fear, the gospel offers a sense of joy that, even when it is juxtaposed with suffering, cannot be destroyed. In a world that majors in confrontation and violence, the gospel holds up the vision of mutuality and reconciliation. In a world that no one understands even after scholars have explained its parts and processes, the gospel celebrates a sense of mystery, which does not explain what we do not know, but helps us to know and to interpret what we do not know in a new light. The gospel focuses the mystery in a human life, the man Jesus of Nazareth, by whose person and work the mystery is illuminated. In light of him, the mystery known to all people of every culture and religion is revealed as personal, relational, compassionate, transforming, and present in the commonplace events of life. The ministry of the church is not to create that sense of mystery or to bring the mystery to people who reside outside the environs of its message and ministry. The mission task of the church is to proclaim the identity of the One with whom all people daily have to do, and to invite them to share the ministry of the believing community.

The ministry of the church is *the science of theology*. In all that the church does, it speaks implicitly or explicitly about God. Whether it speaks about God in the faith and witness of the Christian individual or in the corporate life of the community, it belongs to the ministry of the church to criticize and to revise its theological vocabulary and categories in the light of its norm and of the world in which the church lives. The science of theology is related to, but not identical with, theology as the individual and corporate witness of the church. The science of theology represents the intellectual activity that undergirds, tests, and authenticates theological expression in all forms of the church's ministry. It admits, on the one hand, to the humanity of the theological enterprise. Theology is a human work, susceptible to all the limitations of finitude. No theology ever represents the final or perfect statement of the gospel. On the other hand, theology confesses to its own accountability to God. It is the critical, continuing dialogue of the believing community with the sources and context of the gospel: the Bible, the history of Christian thought, the experience of the community, other expressions of human creativity in the culture of which the church is a part, and the various religions and competing philosophies of life.

The science of theology is the intellectual process by which the church takes its own measure and faces itself with the question of truth, measuring its action, its language about God, against its existence as the church.[27] Theology guides the language and categories of the church by constantly reminding the church that all doctrines and creeds are limited and partial, and thus true and serviceable only by virtue of the grace of God. Theology accompanies the language and categories employed by the church by constantly holding them under the judgment and promise of their norm, the revelation of God in Jesus Christ. "Has Christian language its source in Him?" Barth asks. "Does it lead to Him? Does it conform to Him? . . . Thus as Biblical theology, theology is the question as to the foundation, as practical theology it is the question as to the aim, as dogmatic theology it is the question as to the content, of the language peculiar to the Church."[28]

There has never been a nontheological period in church history. In some manner and to some degree, the science of theology has always and everywhere been pursued as a ministry of importance in the Christian church. The New Testament does not use the word *theology*, but the process of critical reflection whereby the language and categories of faith are tested and shaped in the light of their norm is present throughout. The entire New Testament bears witness to the theological activity of the earliest Christian community as it sought to state the meaning and legitimacy of certain formative events surrounding the person of Jesus of Nazareth in the light of its own experience of the gospel and the world in which it lived.

The Reformed tradition has consistently emphasized the importance of the science of theology. It has considered the task of articulating the Christian faith in intelligible and systematic ways to be of primary importance for the integrity of the existence of the church. There is great variety in Reformed theologies and considerable latitude in interpretive styles, but certain discernible emphases are to be found in Reformed theologies that may (and may not) distinguish them from theologies of other traditions.[29] Reformed theologians have sought to build on the theological work of the past, accepting the validity of the creedal formulations of the ancient catholic church—the Apostles' Creed, the Nicene and Chalcedonian definition of the person of Jesus Christ—and working within the context of the issues raised by the Reformed confessions of the sixteenth and seventeenth centuries. Furthermore, Reformed theology is theocentric; it is centered on God as the triune God. Reformed theology is biblical in the sense that it understands its task to be one of clarifying and focusing the message of the Bible in the context of the contemporary situation. Reformed theology stresses the sovereignty of God and the divine initiative in the procurement and appropriation of salvation. It has sought to underscore the infinite qualitative distinction between the Creator and the creature, between the independence and freedom of God and the dependent, contingent existence of human beings and the world of nature. Reformed theology is concerned with ethics, the practical consequences of Christian faith in God for personal and societal life, and with the integration of the whole person, mind and emotions, in the praise and service of God.

To say that there is a crisis of belief in modern times is not to be unnecessarily alarmist about the contemporary situation. Each new generation constructs its own crisis of belief in relation to the particular intellectual and historical circumstances by which it is constituted. It does mean, however, that no one generation has the luxury of simply accepting and repeating the theology of the past if that generation is to minister to that crisis of belief. The science of theology, like all other forms of the church's ministry, stands in constant need of criticism, correction, and reformation if it is to proclaim, explicate, and apply the gospel to the contemporary situation. The ministry of the science of theology "is a singularly beautiful and joyful science" that must be undertaken willingly and cheerfully by the church in every generation if it is to bear convincing witness to Jesus Christ.[30]

Thus, *the ministry of the church is prayer.* The church is utterly dependent upon God for its existence, maintenance, and efficacy. There is no form or function of the church that is self-sufficient and self-validating.

Prayer is inseparable from action. In its praying, the church acts; as it acts, the church prays. Prayer is the movement of the Creator to the creature, and from the creature to the Creator, by which the ministry of the church is nourished and corrected. Prayer is occasioned not by the human quest for God but by the divine initiative whereby God justifies, sanctifies, adopts, and calls a people to be God's own.

> For in Christ he offers all happiness in place of our misery, all wealth in place of our neediness; in him he opens to us the heavenly treasures that our whole faith may contemplate his beloved Son, our whole expectation depend upon him, and our whole hope cleave to and rest in him. . . . after we have been instructed by faith to recognize

> that whatever we need and whatever we lack is in God, and in our
> Lord Jesus Christ . . . it remains for us to seek in him, and in prayers
> to ask of him, what we have learned to be in him.[31]

Otherwise, the treasure would be neglected and remain buried and hidden in the earth. Therefore, prayer like faith is a gift of God. Even as God stoops to our weakness and seals the witness of the gospel in our hearts, so God also raises up our spirits to dare to express our wishes in prayer.

Prayer may be spoken or unspoken, disciplined or spontaneous, but it is neither the occasional breathing of the soul nor the private gasping of the heart. Prayer is an ongoing ministry of the whole community of faith, which sometimes is expressed in the life of the individual and at other times in corporate worship, by which the church thanks God for grace already received and intercedes with God for the same grace in the present and future. In its praying, the church acknowledges that its existence, maintenance, and efficacy depend on God's grace alone, which it does not and cannot merit, and which comes only as a gift from God's hand.

The church is not timid but bold in prayer, confident that its prayers are heard, expecting its prayers to be answered. Karl Barth puts the church's confidence and expectation in prayer in an interesting way. "In prayer," he says, "the community keeps God to His Word, which is the promise of His faithfulness as the Word which calls, gathers, unbuilds and commissions it."[32] In so saying, Barth means that the life and ministry of the church belong to God. It is God's cause, not ours. Thus, the church has every right to expect that God will be faithful to God's Word, that the church which belonged to God yesterday will belong to God today and tomorrow as well. In prayer, the church lays claim to the faithfulness of God, thrusting itself and its ministry on God's faithful and provident care, and holding God to God's Word.

The ministry of prayer is not simply a matter of the interior life of the church, but an act of witness to the world. Prayer creates in history a fact or an event, which stands alongside other facts and events, that speaks to the world and has significance for the world, whether the world listens and hears or not. The fact that there exists in history a community in which people acknowledge their absolute dependence upon God—thanking God for past grace and interceding with God for future mercy, keeping God to God's Word and seeking to accomplish something in the world—testifies to what God has done and is doing to renovate the fallen world. In a sense, the church goes before the world when it prays, lifting it into God's presence in thanksgiving and intercession and representing to it in a provisional yet authentic way God's will for the entire creation.

The ministry of the church is the cure of souls, or pastoral care. At times, the cure of souls, or pastoral care as it is often called, is delegated to certain persons who possess peculiar sensitivity, talent, and training, be they ordained or unordained. The insights and techniques of psychology and psychiatry have enriched the ministry of the cure of souls with their knowledge of the art of healing. The cure of souls, however, is the ministry of the whole church, for which no Christian can escape responsibility. The church welcomes all forms of assistance from the help-ing sciences, but it never equates its ministry with therapy. The ministry of the cure of souls includes a ministry of referral of troubled people to those equipped with clinical training, but the church's task is different from that of the clinician. The primary task of the church is to proclaim, explicate, and apply the gospel in the ministry of the cure of souls.

> Everything depends upon its fidelity in doing what it does in this understanding. If it knows its own business and acts accordingly, there can be no fear of its becoming a superfluous religious duplication of the neutral science and art, and it will have both in its own narrower circle and in the world around the power of a sign of salvation and witness of the kingdom which only the community can set up.[33]

The cure of souls is compassionate concern for the individual personal exis-tence of particular human beings within and without the church. In biblical lan-guage, the term *soul* means the whole person, whose existence is grounded in God's will, whose identity is the gift of God's love, and whose destiny is guaranteed by God's promised faithfulness. The cure of souls has to do with concern for the indi-vidual in the light of God's will, God's love, and God's destiny within which the individual is held. It is God who is primarily concerned with people, and who is ultimately committed to them, but in God's service the church has been given a corresponding human concern and commitment, the care of one for the other.

Like the other Reformers, John Calvin found in the New Testament the pat-tern of the mutual ministry, which for him was the pattern for the ministry of the church. Calvin considered mutual confession, admonition, correction, con-solation, and edification to be the ordinary activity of Christian people: "Thus, the ecclesiastical importance given to laymen by Calvin lies not only in the elder-ship, with its disciplinary authority, but also in the enlisting of all in a lively atten-tion to each other's spiritual state and needs."[34] Calvin himself was a pastor and wrote the office of pastor into his church structure, not to suggest that the cure of souls was to be limited to the clerical office but in order that the common min-istry of the church might not be without representative leadership. Calvin's per-sonal correspondence is full of pastoral counsel, rebuke, encouragement, guidance, consolation, and appeals for reconciliation to those who were alien-ated. Sometimes people with whom he corresponded reciprocated with their own pastoral criticisms of him. "Still I take it kindly of you to exhort me to modera-tion," Calvin wrote to Francis Dryander, who had complained of Calvin's uncon-trolled anger, adding, "I am perfectly aware that my temper is naturally inclined to be violent" (November 1557).[35] Such frank and patient interchange illustrates Calvin's pastoral view of the church as the environment in which mutual con-fession and correction are possible without bitterness or recrimination.

In the ministry of the cure of souls, each Christian claims the ministry of the whole church by inviting others into a mutual relationship of openness, trust, and fidelity; by listening and speaking; by proclaiming, explicating, and applying the gospel, both verbally and nonverbally; and by being receptive to the witness to the gospel borne by the other person's life. So to serve God and others is to obey and to testify to God's will for all people, and thus to share in what God has done and is doing to renovate the fallen world.

The ministry of the church is the raising up of illustrative personal examples of Christian faith and life. In the early church, and in all subsequent periods of the church's life, there have emerged individuals who, by the uncommon depth of their faith or by the unique integrity of their witness, have provided representative leadership to the community as a whole. Sometimes these influential persons were accorded high office in the life of the church, while in other cases they had no official function at all. More important than office or function was the general perception of the community that these persons manifested in their lives with exemplary clarity that which was common to all Christians, and that the life and ministry of the whole community was somehow blessed by their presence. This may well explain the inclusion of the phrase, "to another faith by the same spirit" in the Pauline catalog of the gifts given by God to the church in 1 Corinthians 12:9—the exemplary depth and inordinate power of faith represented in certain individuals within the community, by which its life was blessed. The witness of these extraordinary individuals from the beginning of church history has enriched the church's understanding of the gospel, sharpened its thinking, stimulated its witness in the world, and provided the critical ferment that issues in reformation. A basic form of the ministry of the church in every generation, therefore, is the development and nurture of these representative examples of Christian faith and life.

This ministry is not without its history of error or devoid of contemporary temptations. As far back as the first and second centuries, martyrs were held in high honor in the church. Their cults grew rapidly in the fourth and fifth centuries. After the centuries of persecution were over, converts flooded the church and often transferred to the martyrs of the past some of the reverence they had given, as well as the attributes and powers they had ascribed, to the gods of paganism.[36] The relics of the martyrs were collected and cherished; their tombs became the object of pious pilgrimages; they were appealed to in prayer to intercede with God on behalf of the ordinary believer; they were believed to work miracles, heal diseases, protect cities, and enhance commerce. To the martyrs were added Christians of exemplary lives, especially ascetics, as those through whom prayers might be made. The regularization of the process of canonization did not occur until the twelfth century, when Pope Alexander III decreed that in the future none should be enrolled among the saints without papal consent, but the process was already in being years before through popular consensus in the church at large.

The Reformers often excoriated the abuse associated with the process of canonization and the veneration of saints on the basis of their conviction that it robbed Christ of the honor of mediation. Lutherans did not jettison the theory and practice of canonization altogether. They cut back on the cult but preserved parts of the calendar of saints. Calvinists did not deny the existence of exemplary lives in the history of the church, but they believed that the saints departed were engaged with God and not with the vicissitudes of life on earth. Calvin called the attempt to gain access to God through the saints "the height of stupidity, not to say madness." He concluded that "those who account Christ's intercession worthless unless George and Hippolytus and such specters come forward leave nothing for Christ to do."[37]

To be sure, the temptation before the Reformed community today is not the reinstitution of canonization or the veneration of saints, but it well may be the self-promotion of its prominent figures who call attention to themselves by their dramatic style and hot pursuit of their own careers, "perhaps even beating their fellow-servants and eating and drinking with the drunken" (Matt. 24:49).[38] If men and women who are particularly gifted are successful in resisting this temptation, they will yet have to devise strategies for dealing with the threats to their integrity that come with popular acclaim, idolization, hero worship, and public prominence. There is always the danger that the cause of Jesus Christ will be associated too closely with the faith, conduct, and winsome personality of certain individuals, obscuring their pretensions, excusing their arrogance, and hiding their sin. For this reason, the church does well to limit the time and sphere of operation of the gifted individual in its midst. It must never fail to concentrate on its ministry of developing and nurturing other exemplary figures, that the history of error may not be repeated in different guise but with equal devastation to the witness of the gospel in the church today.

This form of the church's ministry does not contradict the priesthood of all believers, nor the equality of all Christians before God, nor the universal need of God's grace. It simply amounts to the frank admission that the church is not uniform, "that the Holy Spirit is not a friend of too doctrinaire democracy,"[39] that God chooses to raise up certain individuals to serve the community as models or examples, their witness being more clear and comprehensible than others. In these persons, the church sees, however partially, the fullness to which all are called. The excellence of one may be personal warmth, of another an unusually fine mind, of another great wisdom, of another uncommon administrative skill, and of another deep piety. None is full or perfect, but each bears a particular witness to Jesus Christ for which the church should be thankful. The ministry of the church is to develop and to nurture these exceptional examples of faith and witness for the greater integrity of its own existence and for its outreach to the world.

The ministry of the church is in the ministry of its diaconate, the ministry of serving to people in need. The ministry of service was acknowledged very early in the history of the church. We read in Acts 6 of the solemn process in the infant Jerusalem fellowship whereby seven persons, identified by name, were set apart for the ministry (*diakonia*) of providing for widows and waiting on tables, thus enabling the apostles to devote themselves to prayer and the ministry of the Word. These persons were not yet expressly called deacons. In fact, in most of the New Testament, the word *diakonia* refers to the ministry of service incumbent on all Christians. It was not until the second century that the office of deacon attached liturgical responsibilities to the social function for which the diaconate was created. Martin Bucer in Strasbourg and John Calvin in Geneva sought to recover the understanding of the diaconate in the early church by redefining it in terms of the ministry of service and giving it place in the polity of the church.

In one sense, all forms of the church's ministry are forms of service, but there is good reason specifically to identify service as a form of ministry. In the other forms of ministry, service often is obscured or lost from view altogether. The witness of a powerful preacher, a learned theologian, or an influential lay leader of the church, for example, is easily compromised by personal ambition and public acclaim, so that the ministry of service is often overwhelmed by the pride of the practitioner. The diaconate of the church cannot be subordinated quite so readily when it is established as a basic form of the church's ministry. Caring for the sick, the weak, the mentally ill, and the emotionally distressed; providing for orphans, widows, the bereaved, and the aged; and helping the prisoner, the refugee, the hungry, and the homeless constitute one of the primary tasks of the church, which is often accomplished without fanfare or recognition in simple acts of compassion.

In the ministry of service, the church identifies itself with the plight of the suffering, afflicted, powerless, and abused people of society, who live in relative obscurity on the margins of the common life, and who represent a problem for the society as a whole. The ministry of service bears witness to the fact that these wounded persons, who present such a burden to society at large, are nevertheless children of God, brothers and sisters of Christ, in the serving of whom Christ himself is served. The existence of the diaconate as a basic form of ministry proclaims that these people are wanted and not simply tolerated by the church. The diaconate is the proclamation, explication, and application of the gospel in concrete and particular terms in relation to human need that saves everything else the church thinks and says from sentimentality.

Of increasing concern, both to those committed to the church's ministry to people in need and to those committed to the separation of church and state, are proposals to increase the availability of public funds to churches. Division of opinion over this issue threatens to reopen old wounds between races and classes, threatening the atmosphere of goodwill and cooperation that characterizes current interchurch relations. Many African American pastors have their offices "across the tracks" and drive past blocks of shotgun shacks to meet with white ministers, whose offices are surrounded by golf courses, gated communities, and many other accoutrements of affluence. Many urban black ministers, confronted daily by the needs of the poor, are more willing to consider government assistance for their programs than their white suburban counterparts. "These children are hungry," said one pastor in a poor urban neighborhood. "Now I am a minister, but if I have to remove the Bible, remove the cross from the wall, remove the Ten Commandments to get that government money, I'll do it. If God is in me, that's good enough." It is not clear, however, that the church is any less immune to the politics of self-interest than the government, nor is it clear that the availability of public money would not pit one religion against another, unravel decades of efforts to build interracial and interfaith relationships, and ultimately exclude minority faiths. This is not only an issue being raised in the United States, but it is a subject of heated debate in other countries as well. The invasion of the ministry of the church by government always places the prophetic independence of the church at risk. In whatever country this issue is raised, both church and state must be on guard against the diminution of the freedom of each from the undue influence of the other.

The ministry of service, however, cannot be defined simply in terms of helping people who are injured, ill, deprived, or oppressed. This ministry is never adequately undertaken unless it is also understood that the human need to which the church seeks to be responsive grows out of systemic disorders in the society at large, by which the church itself is implicated. Thus, the diaconate of the church requires that critical attention be given to the social, economic, and political disorders in society, as well as the church's commitment to alter those forms of social injustice that cause people to suffer. "The diaconate and the Christian community become dumb dogs, and their service a serving of the ruling powers," writes Karl Barth, "if they are afraid to tackle at their social roots the evils by which they are confronted in detail."[40]

The diaconate of the church may be given representative leadership by certain persons or groups of people within the community, but the ministry of service is a ministry of the whole church and cannot finally be delegated. The church is called to undertake large projects in the name of Christian service whenever these projects have promise, but there is also a great deal that can be done by way of a quiet, personal diaconate among Christians, and between Christians and non-Christians: simple acts of kindness, visiting the sick, practicing forgiveness, working for reconciliation, and caring for the lonely in the home, in hospitals and nursing homes, and in countless other places. The church fulfills the ministry of service both in the diaconate of its corporate life, and in the diaconate of its individual members.

The ministry of the church is prophetic action, the action of word or deed that is based on insights into the meaning of events, relationships, and social systems, in the light of their positive or negative relationship to what God has done and is doing to renovate the fallen world.

The prophet in the Old Testament was not only a seer, one who was able to preview and predict the future. The prophet was a theologian of history, who interpreted the meaning of historical events, relationships, and systems, both of Israel's history and that of the contemporary world, in the light of their positive or negative relationship to the purposes of God. In the New Testament, we read that there were male and female prophets in the early church, some of whom were considered to be authentic and some of whom were not (Matt. 24:11). In fact, prophecy is the only gift of the Spirit to the church mentioned in all lists

(Rom. 12:6; 1 Cor. 12:10; Eph. 4:11). The exact nature of prophecy in the early church is not completely clear. It would be a mistake simply to equate early Christian prophecy with the activity of Old Testament prophets. Prophecy in the early church may well have involved a more ecstatic or emotional response to the activity of the Spirit in contemporary circumstances. We do know from 1 Corinthians 14, however, that prophecy in the early church was clearly distinguished from speaking in tongues, that the Spirit at work in the prophet's life did not overwhelm the person's ability to control the prophetic utterance, that prophecy was intended to be understood and that others in the community were to "weigh what is said" (14:29), and that prophecy was intended to edify the community and to confirm the apostolic testimony represented by Paul. These are important clues as to the nature of prophecy in the early church. Whatever else prophecy may have been, it represented special insight into the unique understanding and interpretation of the divine will and activity in the church and the world.

John Calvin affirmed that the Old Testament prophets were interpreters of the law, faithful interpreters of history, and foretellers of things to come, upon whose testimony, along with the apostles, the church was founded. He also included prophets along with apostles, evangelists, pastors, and teachers, in his summary of the scriptural offices of the ministry in the church. He believed, however, that of these, only pastors and teachers have an ordinary office in the church, that the Lord raised up apostles, prophets, and evangelists only "at the beginning of his Kingdom, and now and again revives them as the need of the times demand."[41] Yet Calvin's deep concern for the integrity of the Christian life, the calling of the Christian individual, and the transformation of culture is good evidence of his commitment to the prophetic ministry of the church. John Leith argues that "John Calvin stands out in the history of the church as one who was more vividly aware than almost any other of the mighty working of God in human history and of God's call to his people for service in the world."[42] Calvin's intention in Geneva was not simply the salvation of individuals but the transformation of the city into a holy community in which God was worshiped and served. Calvin's vision of the holy commonwealth on earth was never fully realized, for the reality and power of human sin render all human achievements partial and provisional at best, but his vision lives on in the conviction of Reformed communities that history is the scene of the divine activity and that the church is called to bear witness to that fact.

The church undertakes its prophetic ministry today when it makes public pronouncements concerning the meaning of current events, contemporary relationships, and social systems, in their positive or negative connection to the purposes and activity of God. Public pronouncements are means by which the church seeks to create and nurture a Christian conscience concerning social, economic, political, personal, and relational issues on the basis of the scriptural clues that point to God's renovating activity in the world. These pronouncements represent a form of the proclamation, explication, and application of the gospel to the particular circumstances of contemporary life, whereby the church identifies, investigates, analyzes, and interprets these circumstances with reference to the Word of God.

Public pronouncements are as dangerous for the ministry of the church as they are necessary to its witness to the gospel. The danger is that they will oversimplify both the issue to which they refer and the divine activity to which they are responsible, thus trivializing the ministry of the church. Some contemporary issues are clearer than others and call for forthright statements of the will of God. The issue of the racial segregation of Christian churches, for example, as well as the marginalization of certain church members on account of their age, sex, or sexual orientation, clearly calls for the church's witness to the inclusiveness of Christ's church. Most issues, however, are more complex and cannot be so simply addressed. There is often no single interpretation of the facts that is completely adequate, no one solution that can be honestly affirmed to be the will of God, and thus no universally normative Christian response. Seldom is the church given such awareness of the divine intention and activity as to justify the assertion that a particular policy or political candidate is in accord with the will of God. The danger is that the church will confuse social or political ideology with the divine will and proclaim it as gospel to the world. Reformed Christians have long been aware of the fact that councils, committees, judicatories, and all other ecclesiastical bodies can and often do err. Thus, they have learned to respect and to listen to the public pronouncements of the church, conscious that they represent the considered opinion of a particular body of believers at one place and time. They also retain the right and responsibility to evaluate, criticize, disagree, and reject such pronouncements as do not appear to reflect an adequate understanding either of the contemporary historical issue or the purposes of God.

The prophetic ministry of the church is also undertaken by representative or symbolic action. At times, the church takes the initiative, intervening in the course of events with its personnel, finances, and property to bear witness to what God has done and is doing to renovate the fallen world. Churches regularly invest themselves, for example, in housing projects for the poor and elderly, in alcohol and drug rehabilitation programs, in counseling services, in the struggle for justice and world peace, and in other forms of action. Sometimes the church recognizes in the work of other organizations, public and private, a kindred spirit or common commitment, and grants to these nonconfessional groups its encouragement and support. The church, confident that it has no monopoly on the Holy Spirit, is encouraged by the existence and success of all groups or organizations that labor for justice, freedom, reconciliation, and peace in the world. It often gives its moral and financial support to groups and organizations that share neither its history nor its creed but that do share its commitments to those essential qualities and characteristics of life in this world that being human requires. But the church must never simply equate its prophetic ministry with the existence or activity of any other group or organization. It must never confuse the gospel with a political panacea, a social program, or a particular human agent of either. "There is no Church, in any sense of the word, apart from human action, but the response of the Church to the community is with a divine purpose."[43] It is not called to replicate the role of other groups or organizations. The church is called to proclaim, explicate, and apply the gospel in and through the ministry of prophetic words and deeds.

The ministry of the church is to pursue and promote genuine human fellowship among people. The church does not create fellowship. Fellowship is both God's gift to the church and a basic form of its ministry. When the church establishes fellowship among people, it bears witness to the being and nature of the triune God. It testifies to the faith that binding love, human interrelatedness, and community are rooted and grounded in the Godhead; that God is the one whose love binds loved ones together, who wills that all men and women should live in community, and who gives fellowship among people as God's good gift. Furthermore, when the church establishes fellowship, it bears witness to the fellowship of Christ with his church and to the general fellowship between God and all creation. Trusting that God has done and is doing what it takes to restore the fractured creation to mutual fellowship, the church invites all people to share in a common life, binding them together as they have never been bound before in unity and community.

This ministry of inviting and binding is fundamental to all forms of the church's ministry, but it is itself one of those basic forms of ministry, in the undertaking of which the church bears witness to the gospel. The fellowship of Christian people does not obscure or obliterate but rather affirms diversity and difference, except where diversity and difference are oppressive and dehumanizing. It includes people of all nations without trying to erase the differences between them. It establishes across national boundaries an international community in which people of all nations meet and find in their fellowship their primary loyalty, with reference to which all other loyalties are judged and affirmed. Likewise, Christian fellowship includes people of various racial, cultural, sexual, and economic orientations, without obscuring or obliterating the rich, humanizing diversity they represent. The church does not appropriate or legitimate differences between people, particularly when they enslave people, nor does it consider these differences to be normative for its own fellowship. The church is called to witness to the restorative activity of God in history by testifying not to equality but to justice—the mutual fellowship of diverse peoples who are noticed, understood, and taken seriously in all their particularity in the fellowship of Christian community. In so doing, the church proclaims, explicates, and applies the gospel of God.

The ministry of fellowship is currently in danger of dissolution due to divisions within the churches on social issues, particularly issues of human sexuality. Protestant denominations and their member churches often find the ministry of fellowship caught between the freedom of the individual conscience on the one hand and the corporate mind of the church on the other. What is one to do, what is a church to do, when sincerely held convictions divide the body of Christ and make the ministry of fellowship all but impossible?

There is no easy answer to this question, at least none that will preclude the further fragmentation of the church. Protestantism is itself a child of division,

and fragmentation has marked its life ever since. In part, the tendency to frag-
ment is due to the Protestant conviction concerning how the Bible is to be read.
The Reformers, some more reluctantly than others, accepted the risk and reality
of disunity as preferable to any institution or authority within with the power to
dictate how the Bible was to be read. The conviction that the Holy Spirit speaking through Scripture is the ultimate authority, and that all believers, being
priests, are obligated to take responsibility for their own faith is the source both
of Protestant strength and Protestant weakness.

What this means for contemporary church life is that fragmentation always
lurks in the shadows of the ministry of fellowship. In *The Book of Church Order*,
the form of government of the former Presbyterian Church in the United States,
candidates for ordination to the ministry, and for the offices of elder and deacon
as well, were asked, "Do you promise subjection to your brethren in the Lord?"
That question is no longer used in Presbyterian communities today to my knowledge, but perhaps it ought to be since it places the unity of the church and the
ministry of fellowship at the top of the ecclesial agenda. The problem with the
question is that it fails to acknowledge the Achilles' heel of Protestantism, which
is the problem of authority.

Somehow the church must make its way through this minefield by means of
such ordinary Christian virtues as the love of the neighbor, honest dialogue,
mutual respect, and the grace of forgiveness, acknowledging that the boundaries
of the people of God are very wide and inclusive. This will not preclude the further fragmentation of the church. Issues of truth and righteousness may continue
to provoke divisions within the body. What it will do is to serve as a reminder of
the ministry of fellowship as the calling to seek the unity of the church in bonds
of peace while the church remains willing to risk everything for the sake of truth
and justice when so led by the Holy Spirit.

TO BE A PILGRIM

No book on the Reformed doctrine of the church can have a conclusion, even
though all books must come to an end, for the final affirmation to be made is
that the story is not over and will not be over until God's will for the creation has
been accomplished. The story of the church, which began at creation, which was
fulfilled in Jesus Christ, and which now includes you and me, is a continuing
story. We are participants today in this continuing story of God's unparalleled
renovation of the world. Various images have been used to suggest that the church
is on a journey, that, having begun, the church has not yet arrived at its destina-
tion. The image of the pilgrimage has been suggestive since Abraham went out
from Ur of the Chaldees in response to God's call, "not knowing where he was
to go" (Heb. 11:8). Augustine referred to Christian existence as a "pilgrimage by
faith,"[44] and Calvin used the image with specific reference to the life of the
church. Christ teaches us, Calvin wrote, "to travel as pilgrims in this world that

our celestial heritage may not perish or pass away."[45] In 1684, John Bunyan, who had been greatly influenced by Calvinism, wrote his famous *Pilgrim's Progress,* a portion of which became a familiar hymn in Reformed circles. In the original, one of its verses reads:

> Who would true Valour see,
> Let him come hither;
> One here will Constant be,
> Come Wind, come Weather,
> There's no Discouragement,
> Shall make him once Relent,
> His first avow'd Intent,
>   To be a Pilgrim.[46]

The image of the pilgrim continues to be suggestive for the existence of the church today. To be a pilgrim is to be on the move from somewhere to somewhere, oriented by a sense of purpose and direction. To be a pilgrim is to be at home in the world yet at the same time to be a stranger to it. It is to live as a responsible citizen of the cities of the earth yet always on the lookout for "the city which has foundations, whose builder and maker is God" (Heb. 11:10). It is to be on the move with fellow travelers from birth to death in a pilgrim band, thankful that God has left no one to travel the road alone. To be a pilgrim is to follow Jesus Christ, the pioneer of our salvation. It is to celebrate, bear witness to, and participate in all that God has done and is doing to renovate the fallen world, trusting in God's sovereignty and clinging to God's mercy. John Calvin, in a poem entitled "The Church as Pilgrim," summarizes what it means to be a pilgrim, and with his words we rest our case.

> Let us remember:
> However low the church's outward state,
> It shines in inward beauty;
> Though shaken upon earth,
>
> In heaven it is firmly seated;
> Though in the world's sight it lies maimed and fallen,
> Before God and His angels it stands whole and flourishes;
> Though wretched after the flesh,
> In the spirit it abounds in spiritual blessedness.
>
> Even so, when Christ lay lowly in the manger,
> In the clouds the angels sang His loftiness;
> In heaven the star witnessed to His glory;
> The wise men from a far-off land felt His power.
>
> When he fasted in the wilderness,
> Struggled against the mockeries of Satan,
> Sweated unto death,
> Still were angels ministering to Him.

When He was about to be imprisoned,
By His voice alone He drove back His enemies.

While He hung upon the cross,
The sun by its darkness proclaimed Him King of all,
The opened graves confessed Him Lord of death and life.

Now if we see Christ
In His body troubled by the proud insults of the wicked,
Oppressed by their savage tyranny,
Exposed to their abuse,
Driven to and fro by their violence:
However insolent, none of these things can frighten us.

Rather let us ponder
That the church is ordained,
So long as it is pilgrim in the world,
To fight under a continual cross. [47]

Epilogue: The Church
That People Love

When all is said and done, one of the best indicators of a church's faithfulness and effectiveness is the extent to which people who belong to it love it. Attendance and giving records go up and down. Many relatively inconsequential factors influence both. Likewise, the public influence of the church, the place assigned to it by contemporary society, its fiscal circumstance and physical presence tell us very little about the true state of the church at any particular time. If one wishes to get to the heart of the matter, one must look beneath the surface of the church's institutional life in an effort to discern whether and to what extent people genuinely love it.

Love of the church, passion for the seat of worship of the Lord God, is a very ancient human experience. Psalm 84, for instance, expresses without apology or embarrassment the Old Testament love of the house of God, as do many New Testament texts. As the pilgrim approaches the hallowed city of Jerusalem and catches sight of the mount upon which Solomon's great edifice rests, the sheer joy of it all literally explodes into a shout from the heart: "How lovely is your dwelling place, O Lord of hosts!"

In the worship life of Israel, that love-shout would have been sung as well in the gathered congregation, set to a popular tune long since lost, named "Gittith." Over the course of time, many modern settings have been inspired by the psalm, perhaps because there is something about its unguarded emotion that cannot resist the setting into song. The most distinguished, of course, is Brahms's *German Requiem,* the opening theme of which is as familiar to contemporary worshipers as "Gittith" was to the congregation of old Israel. "How lovely is your dwelling place, O Lord of hosts!"

But it was not the building alone, magnificent though it was, that elicited this song of love. It was what the building stood for and called to mind. It was the thought of what went on there Sabbath after Sabbath, festival after festival: the worship of the Holy One, teaching and learning the things that pertain to God, the various rituals that surrounded birth and death and most everything else in between. It was those historical signs, manifestations, and narrative portrayals of what we have been calling God's unparalleled renovation of the world. The building, the place that centered these memories in a tradition of believing, was understood to be God's gracious gift, and people were unfeignedly thankful.

What I am getting to is the fact that churches, like people, have distinct personalities. Some are strong in numbers, some weak. Some are outgoing and welcoming of the stranger, while others are more reserved and formal in their invitation to friendship. But the most interesting and intriguing thing about churches of every size and style is that some touch people's hearts, while others do not. What makes the difference? What are the marks or characteristics of the church that people love?

First, a partial but not inconsequential answer to these questions is sentiment. The church that people love is the church to which people are vitally attached by bonds of sentiment, and of these we need not be ashamed. Sentiment is not sentimentality. Sentiment is idea colored by emotion; it is feeling that has its reasons. As such, it is evidence of the self-authenticating presence and activity of the Holy Spirit in and upon the life of the church. "True religion, in great part," said Jonathan Edwards, "consists in the affections . . . in vigorous and lively actings of the inclinations and will of the soul, or the fervent exercises of the heart."[1]

The bonds of sentiment are drawn tight upon the heart, for instance, when the significant occasions of life are corporately consecrated and lifted to God in prayer. To grow up in a church; to worship and to experience the grace of God within its walls; to dedicate or rededicate a life to Jesus Christ in its youth fellowship or prayer group; to marry, to present children for baptism, to gather at time of death in its sanctuary is to be provided over time with those ideas colored by emotions that make the difference between a church to which people nominally belong and the church that people love.

Second, the church that people love will likely be the church that expects things of them. We have often been told that one of the reasons that conservative churches are growing while so many of the churches of the Protestant mainline are declining in membership is that conservative churches ask and expect things of people whereas the more established churches do not. That estimate of the situation may or may not be true, but it does serve as a reminder that one of the greatest mistakes any church can make is to try to protect people from the very real cost of Christian discipleship.

The time has come for American mainline Protestantism to serve notice to its people that this matter of being and staying Christian in the contemporary world is increasingly complex; that the cultural cards are no longer stacked in favor of the church in a way that privileges Christian faith, values, and life; that time, energy, and money, as well as intellectual rigor and moral courage, will be required if the church is not only to survive but to be an active "player" in the determination and construction of the common good.

After all, unless we have been cruelly deceived, the church is the Master's business, the provisional representation of what God intends for the entire creation, an instrument of God's unparalleled renovation of the fallen world. The church that people love will likely be the church that considers this business so important and takes its detail so seriously that it asks and expects of people the very best they have to give.

Third, there is little doubt that the church that people love is the church that brings God near and makes God real in their daily lives. God, of course, is near to people and real in their daily lives, whether or not they know it, believe it, feel it, or desire it. And God does not need the church to make it so. But to put things this way does have a way of saying something important about the church that people love. It is a way of admitting that what people want and need from the church, first and foremost, is not more programs and activities to clutter their lives; not more fellowship, or therapy, or musical events, or field trips; not more books to read or more food to eat. All of these things can usually be found elsewhere, often in greater quantity and of higher quality.

What people want from the church before, above, and beyond all else is the reality of the living God, a sense of God's presence and providence in and over their lives. G. K. Chesterton said that nothing is real until it becomes local, and in matters of the spirit, people need help with that. It is not at all obvious that there is a God or that God is both real and local. People today are saying to the church what Phillip said to Jesus. "Show us the Father and we shall be satisfied" (John 14:8). The church that does this will, no doubt, be the church that people love.

Finally, the church that people love is the church that has the spirit of Jesus Christ. Paul said that "anyone who does not have the Spirit of Christ does not belong to him" (Rom. 8:9), and the same is true for the church. Any church that does not have the spirit of Christ does not belong to him. The spirit of Christ I take to be his indomitable love for all sorts and conditions of people; his acute awareness and sympathetic understanding of their weakness and strengths, and of how easily the one can become the other; his critical discernment, which could cut clean through all rationalization and self-deception to bring the reality of a situation to light; the unconditional and unequivocal cast of his forgiveness; his faith in those who had little or no faith in him; his hope for them who had lost all hope; his determination to seek the lost until he found them; his life's intention to heal the sick, to free the captive, to comfort the dying; his resurrection promise made good on the third day. The spirit of Christ is the pressure of his way and will and work, the force of his life, death, and resurrection, on our churchly song, keeping conscience alive and assuring us that truth will not die in the church.

"For I am quite convinced," said John Calvin, "that truth does not die in the church, even though it be oppressed by one council, but is wonderfully preserved by the Lord so that it may rise up and triumph again in its own time. But I deny it to be always the case that an interpretation of Scripture adopted by vote of a council is true and certain."[2] The church was wrong when it justified slavery and segregation with fatally flawed theology. It was wrong when it fought scientific judgments concerning human origins with obscurantist biblical interpretation. It was wrong when it supported the subordination of women to men in society and church. And I do believe that it is wrong today in its judgmental and restrictive attitudes and policies toward gay and lesbian people. But I am greatly comforted by the conviction, so central to Reformed ecclesiology, that truth does not die in the church, that Christ is true though the church be false, that the Easter-earnest has been given the church that his spirit will be raised from the dead and triumph in its own time—that the future belongs to the living God, in other words, and to no one and nothing else. In the final analysis, when all is said and done, it is the church of the living God that is the church that people love.

Notes

Chapter 1

1. John Horgan, "Science Set Free from Truth," *New York Times*, 16 July 1996.
2. Arthur Schlesinger Jr., "History as Therapy: A Dangerous Idea," *New York Times*, 3 May 1996.
3. See Diogenes Allen, "The End of the Modern World," *Christian Scholar's Review*, June 1993, reprinted by the Center of Theological Inquiry.
4. Annie Dillard, *Teaching a Stone to Talk* (New York: Harper & Row, 1982), 40–41.
5. John Polkinghorne, *The Faith of a Physicist* (Minneapolis: Fortress Press, 1996), 76.
6. e e cummings, "the Cambridge ladies who live in furnished souls," *Poems* (New York: Harcourt, Brace & Co., 1954), 58.

Chapter 2

1. Cited by John H. Leith in *An Introduction to the Reformed Tradition* (Atlanta: John Knox Press, 1977), 21–22.
2. John T. McNeill, *Unitive Protestantism* (Richmond: John Knox Press, 1964), 16.
3. Leith, *Introduction to the Reformed Tradition*, 54.

Chapter 3

1. H. Richard Niebuhr, *The Meaning of Revelation* (New York: Macmillan, 1962), 59–60.
2. Cited in John T. McNeill, *Unitive Protestantism* (Richmond: John Knox Press, 1964), 21.
3. Benjamin C. Milner Jr., *Calvin's Doctrine of the Church* (Leiden: E. J. Brill, 1970), 7–9.
4. "The Heidelberg Catechism," in *The Creeds of Christendom*, ed. Philip Schaff (New York: Harper & Brothers, 1905), 3:417.
5. "The Belgic Confession," in Schaff, ed., *Creeds of Christendom*, 3:417.
6. "The Scots Confession," in *The Book of Confessions* (Philadelphia: United Presbyterian Church, n.d.), 3.05.
7. John Calvin, *Commentary on the Book of the Prophet Isaiah*, trans. William Pringle. 4 vols. (Edinburgh: The Calvin Translation Society, 1852). 3: 206.
8. John Calvin, *Institutes of the Christian Religion*, ed. John T. McNeill, trans. Ford Lewis Battles, 4 vols., Library of Christian Classics, vol. 21 (Philadelphia: Westminster Press, 1960), III:20, 44.
9. John Calvin, *Commentary on the Book of Psalms*, trans. John Anderson (Edinburgh: Calvin Translation Society, 1849), 4:358.
10. John Calvin, *Commentaries of the First Book of Moses Called Genesis*, trans. John King (Edinburgh: Calvin Translation Society, 1847), 1:448.

11. Eric Pace, "I. A. Richards," *New York Times*, 8 September 1979, 36.
12. Robert McAfee Brown, *The Ecumenical Revolution* (Garden City, N.Y.: Doubleday, 1967), 273–74.
13. D. M. Baillie, *God Was in Christ* (New York: Charles Scribner's Sons, 1948), 184.

Chapter 4

1. George Gallup Jr. and David Poling, *The Search for America's Faith* (Nashville: Abingdon Press, 1980), 88.
2. Calvin, *Institutes*, 4.1.1.
3. Ibid., 3.11.2.
4. Cyprian, "On the Unity of the Catholic Church," in *Early Latin Theology*, ed. and trans. Stanley Lawrence Greenslade (Philadelphia: Westminster Press, 1960), 127–28.
5. Anders Nygren, *Christ and His Church*, trans. Alan Carlsten (Philadelphia: Westminster Press, 1956), 30.
6. John T. McNeill, *Unitive Protestantism* (Richmond: John Knox Press, 1964), 9.
7. Gregory of Nazianzus, "The Fifth Theological Oration—On the Spirit," in *Christology of the Later Fathers*, ed. Edward Rochie Hardy with Cyril C. Richardson (Philadelphia: Westminster Press, 1954), 206.
8. Philip Schaff, ed., *The Creeds of Christendom* (New York: Harper & Brothers, 1877), 1:26.
9. Gregory of Nazianzus, "Fifth Theological Oration," 196.
10. J. N. D. Kelly, *Early Christian Doctrines*, 2d ed. (London: Adam & Charles Black, 1960), 267.
11. Karl Barth, *Church Dogmatics* (Edinburgh: T. & T. Clark, 1936, 1956, 1958, 1967), I/1:549–50.
12. Paul L. Lehmann, *Ethics in a Christian Context* (New York: Harper & Row, 1963), 49.
13. L. S. Thornton, *The Common Life in the Body of Christ* (London: Dacre Press, 1942), 6.
14. Ibid., 7.
15. McNeill, *Unitive Protestantism*, 22.
16. Lehmann, *Ethics in a Christian Context*, 54–55.
17. Ibid., 101.
18. William Hordern, *New Directions in Theology Today* (Philadelphia: Westminster Press, 1966), 1:112.
19. Barth, *CD* IV/2:642.
20. "The Heidelberg Catechism," *The Book of Confessions* (Philadelphia: United Presbyterian Church, n. d.), 3.05.
21. Jürgen Moltmann, "Is There Life after Death?" in *The End of the World and the Ends of God*, ed. John Polkinghorne and Michael Welker (Harrisburg, Pa.: Trinity Press International, 2000), 254.
22. Robert McAfee Brown, *The Spirit of Protestantism* (New York: Oxford University Press, 1961), 155–56.
23. Paul D. L. Avis, *The Church in the Theology of the Reformers* (Atlanta: John Knox Press, 1981), 95.
24. Calvin, *Institutes* 2:15.6.
25. McNeill, *Unitive Protestantism*, 34.
26. Martin Luther, "The Babylonian Captivity of the Church," in *Luther's Works*, ed. Abdel Ross Wentz, vol. 36 (Philadelphia: Muhlenberg Press, 1959), 116.
27. Martin Luther, "The Private Mass and the Consecration of Priests," *Luther's Works*, vol. 38 (Philadelphia: Fortress Press, 1971), 208–209.

Chapter 5

1. T. S. Eliot, "The Hippopotamus," *Collected Poems, 1909–1950* (New York: Harcourt, Brace & World, 1952), 30.
2. Jaroslav Pelikan, *The Emergence of the Catholic Tradition (100–600)* (Chicago: University of Chicago Press, 1971), 156.
3. Cited in Paul Tillich, *A History of Christian Thought*, 2d ed., rev. and ed. Carl E. Braaten (New York: Harper & Row, 1968), 101.
4. John T. McNeill, *Unitive Protestantism* (Richmond: John Knox Press, 1964), 27.
5. Calvin, *Institutes* 4.1.7.
6. Ibid.
7. John Calvin, *Institutes of the Christian Religion* (Philadelphia: Presbyterian Board of Christian Education, 1930), 4.1.2.
8. E. B. White, *One Man's Meat* (New York: Harper & Row, 1978), 45.
9. Barth, *CD* (1956), IV/1:673.
10. Pelikan, *Catholic Tradition*, 309.
11. Augustine, "Expositions on the Book of Psalms," in *A Select Library of the Nicene and Post-Nicene Fathers of the Christian Church*, ed. Philip Schaff (New York: Christian Literature Company, 1888), 8:473.
12. Augustine, "The Letters of Petilian, The Donatist," in Schaff, ed., *Select Library of the Nicene and Post-Nicene Fathers* (1887), 4:598.
13. Cyril of Jerusalem, "The Catechetical Lectures," in *Cyril of Jerusalem and Nemesius of Emesa*, ed. and trans. William Telfer (Philadelphia: Westminster Press, 1960), 186.
14. Ibid.
15. John H. Leith, ed. *Creeds of the Churches*, 3d ed. (Atlanta: John Knox Press, 1982), 614.
16. Ibid., 631.
17. Ibid., 657.
18. Barth, *CD* (1956), IV/1:714.
19. Ibid., 715.
20. Calvin, *Institutes* 4.1.9.
21. Barth, *CD* (1962), IV/3:764–83.
22. Ibid., 769.
23. Leith, ed., *Creeds of the Churches*, 147.

Chapter 6

1. James Gustafson, *Treasure in Earthen Vessels* (Chicago: University of Chicago Press, 1961), 6. This discussion was influenced by Gustafson's book.
2. Claude Welch, *The Reality of the Church* (New York: Charles Scribner's Sons, 1958), 46.
3. H. Richard Niebuhr, *The Purpose of the Church and Its Ministry* (New York: Harper & Brothers, 1956), 19.
4. Emil Brunner, *The Misunderstanding of the Church*, trans. Harold Knight (London: Lutterworth Press, 1952), 17.
5. Edward A. Dowey Jr., *A Commentary on the Confession of 1967 and an Introduction to the Book of Confessions* (Philadelphia: Westminster Press, 1968), 203.
6. John H. Leith, ed., *Creeds of the Churches*, 3d ed. (Atlanta: John Knox Press, 1982), 179.
7. Ibid., 161.
8. Ibid., 145.
9. Ibid., 182–83.
10. Ibid., 183.

11. J. Douglas Brown, *The Human Nature of Organizations* (New York: American Management Associations, 1973), 5.
12. H. Richard Niebuhr, *The Meaning of Revelation* (New York: The MacMillan Company, 1964), 10.
13. Ibid., 13.
14. Gustafson, *Treasure in Earthen Vessels*, 82.
15. Ibid., 78–80.
16. Barth, *CD* IV/3:812.
17. e e cummings, "The Cambridge ladies who live in furnished souls," *Poems, 1923–1954* (New York: Harcourt, Brace & Co., 1954), 58.
18. John Fry, *The Trivialization of the United Presbyterian Church* (New York: Harper & Row, 1975), 27.
19. Augustine, "On Nature and Grace," in *The Works of Aurelius Augustine*, ed. Marcus Dods (Edinburgh: T. & T. Clark, 1872), 4:262.
20. Peter Brown, *Augustine of Hippo* (Berkeley: University of California Press, 1967), 365. This argument depends on Brown's book.
21. Ibid., 352.

Chapter 7

1. Calvin, *Institutes* 4.11.1.
2. John H. Leith, *An Introduction to the Reformed Tradition* (Atlanta: John Knox Press, 1977), 138.
3. Calvin, *Institutes* 4.4.2.
4. M. Eugene Osterhaven, *The Spirit of the Reformed Tradition* (Grand Rapids: Wm. B. Eerdmans Publishing Co., 1971), 60.
5. Calvin, *Institutes* 4.3.1.
6. John Calvin, "Draft Ecclesiastical Ordinances," in *Calvin: Theological Treatises*, ed. J. K. S. Reid (Philadelphia: Westminster Press, 1960), 58.
7. Ibid., 62–63.
8. H. Richard Niebuhr, *The Purpose of the Church and Its Ministry* (New York: Harper & Brothers, 1956), 64.
9. Calvin, *Institutes* 4.3.2.
10. Ibid., 3.10.6.
11. Emil Brunner, *The Christian Doctrine of the Church, Faith, and the Consummation*, vol. 3 of *Dogmatics* (London: Lutterworth Press, 1962), 43, 99.
12. Ibid., 99.
13. "The Second Helvetic Confession," in *The Book of Confessions* (Philadelphia: United Presbyterian Church, n.d.), 5.153.
14. G. D. Henderson, *Presbyterianism* (Aberdeen, Scotland: Aberdeen University Press, 1954), 54.
15. Calvin, "Draft Ecclesiastical Ordinances," 63.
16. Ibid., 63–64.
17. Ibid., 64.
18. Calvin, *Institutes* 4.10.27–28.
19. Henderson, *Presbyterianism*, 61.
20. James M. Gustafson, "The Voluntary Church: A Moral Appraisal," *Voluntary Associations: A Study of Groups in Free Societies*, ed. D. B. Robertson (Richmond: John Knox Press, 1966), 299–300.
21. John Dillenberger and Claude Welch, *Protestant Christianity* (New York: Charles Scribner's Sons, 1954), 100.
22. Leith, *Introduction to the Reformed Tradition*, 25.

23. George Gallup Jr. and David Poling, *The Search for America's Faith* (Nashville: Abingdon Press, 1980), 146.
24. Cited in Frederick S. Carney, "Associational Thought in Early Calvinism," in D. B. Robertson, ed., *Voluntary Association*, 41.
25. Paul Lehmann, *Ethics in a Christian Context* (New York: Harper & Row, 1963), 83–101.
26. Aristotle, *The Nicomachean Ethics*, trans. H. Rackham (Cambridge, Mass.: Harvard University Press, 1962), 1.2.7.
27. Richard Baxter, *The Reformed Pastor*, ed. John T. Wilkinson (London: Epworth Press, 1939), 47–48.
28. James F. Gustafson, "Political Images of the Ministry," in *The Church, the University, and Social Policy*, ed. Kenneth Underwood, The Danforth Study of Campus Ministries (Middletown, Conn.: Wesleyan University Press, 1969), 2:251. My discussion of the minister as a politician is suggested and influenced by Gustafson's article.
29. Jeffrey K. Hadden, *The Gathering Storm in the Churches* (New York: Doubleday, 1969).
30. Gustafson, "Political Images of the Ministry," 2:252.
31. James F. Gustafson, *Treasure in Earthen Vessels* (Chicago: University of Chicago Press, 1961), 39. This discussion of the church executive is occasioned by Gustafson here and elsewhere.

Chapter 8

1. Barth, *CD* (1962), IV/3:830. The discussion that follows is indebted to Karl Barth's definition of "the ministry of the community" in *CD* IV/3:830–901.
2. "Confession of 1967," *The Book of Confessions* (Philadelphia: United Presbyterian Church, n.d.), 9.32–9.33.
3. W. A. Visser 't Hooft, *The Renewal of the Church* (London: SCM Press, 1956), 124.
4. Barth, *CD* (1962), IV/3:831.
5. Ibid., 838.
6. John H. Leith, ed., *Creeds of the Churches*, 3d ed. (Atlanta: John Knox Press, 1982), 1.
7. Barth, *CD* IV/3:851.
8. Ibid., 865–901.
9. C. Ellis Nelson, *Where Faith Begins* (Richmond: John Knox Press, 1967), 103.
10. Calvin, *Institutes* 4.2.12.
11. Ibid., 4.10.12.
12. John T. McNeill, *The History and Character of Calvinism* (New York: Oxford University Press, 1962), 131.
13. Julius Melton, *Presbyterian Worship in America* (Richmond: John Knox Press, 1967), 15–16.
14. John H. Leith, *An Introduction to the Reformed Tradition* (Atlanta: John Knox Press, 1977), 80.
15. Barth, *CD* IV/3:867.
16. "Theological Declaration of Barmen," *The Book of Confessions* (Philadelphia: United Presbyterian Church, n.d.), 8.11.
17. Barth, *CD* IV/3:871.
18. Leith, *Introduction to the Reformed Tradition*, 217.
19. Perry Miller and Thomas H. Johnson, *The Puritans* (New York: American Book Company, 1938), 701.
20. Barth, *CD* IV/3:871.
21. Paul D. L. Avis, *The Church in the Theology of the Reformers* (Atlanta: John Knox Press, 1981), 167–79.

22. Cited in Avis, *Church in the Theology,* 176.
23. Barth, *CD* IV/3:873.
24. Leith, *Introduction to the Reformed Tradition,* 26.
25. Avis, *Church in the Theology,* 211.
26. Lesslie Newbigin, *The Finality of Jesus Christ* (Richmond: John Knox Press, 1969), 44.
27. Barth, *CD* I/1:2.
28. Ibid., I/1:3.
29. Leith, *Introduction to the Reformed Tradition,* 93–109.
30. Barth, *CD* IV/3:881.
31. Calvin, *Institutes* 3.20.1.
32. Barth, *CD* IV/3:883.
33. Ibid., IV/3:887.
34. McNeill, *History and Character of Calvinism,* 220.
35. Cited in McNeill, *History and Character of Calvinism,* 220–21.
36. Kenneth Scott Latourette, *A History of Christianity* (New York: Harper & Brothers, 1953), 209.
37. Calvin, *Institutes* 3.20.27.
38. Barth, *CD* IV/3:888.
39. Ibid.
40. Barth, IV/3:893.
41. Calvin, *Institutes* 4.3.4.
42. Leith, *Introduction to the Reformed Tradition,* 72.
43. Samuel W. Blizzard, "The Eternal Church in the Changing Community," *Social Progress* 44, no. 7 (March 1954): 5.
44. Augustine, *The City of God,* trans. Marcus Dods (New York: Modern Library, 1950), 483.
45. Calvin, *Institutes* 3.7.4.
46. Cited in Albert Edward Bailey, *The Gospel in Hymns* (New York: Charles Scribner's Sons, 1950), 40.
47. Ford Lewis Battles, trans. and ed., *The Piety of John Calvin* (Grand Rapids: Baker Book House, 1978), 173–74.

Epilogue

1. The Cole Lectures, "Toward the Recovery of Feeling." Cited in *H. Richard Niebuhr: Theology, History, and Culture,* ed. William Stacy Johnson (New Haven, Conn.: Yale University Press, 1996), 44.
2. Calvin, *Institutes* 4.9.13.

Index of Names

Index of Subjects

Anabaptists, 79, 116

Belgic Confession, 20, 139
Belhar Confession, 56
Bible, 18–29, 88–89, 93

church
   apostolic, 52–53, 60–61
   catholic, 58–60
   holy, 57–58
   humanity, 65–82
   marks, 52–61
   necessity of, 32–35
   one, 56–57
   polity, 83–94
   renovation of the world, 22–29
   semantic problem, 50–51
   story of, 17–29
church executive, 102–4
Commission on Faith and Order, 59–60
communion of saints, 40–44
Confession of 1967, 83, 106, 143
Council of Constantinople, 37, 52
Council of Nicaea, 36
covenant, 24–26
creation, 22–23
cross, 28
cure of souls, 122

deacon, 88
diakonia, 48, 87, 125–26
Diet of Speyer, 12
Donatist controversy, 57–58

ecclesia reformata semper reformanda, 82
ecclesiastical docetism, 68–69
elder, 87–88
evangelism, 115
extra ecclesiam nulla salus, 61–64

fall, 23–24
fellowship, 130
filioque, 37

Heidelberg Catechism 20, 42, 139, 140
Holy Spirit, 36

justification, 32–33, 46

koinonia, 38–40

Lord's Supper, 44

minister
   call, 86–87
   politician, 97–102

Pelagian controversy, 79–81
Pentecost, 19, 35, 38
politics, 94–97
postmodernism, 4–6
prayer, 121
preaching, 112–14
priesthood of all believers, 45–48
prophetic action, 127
Protestant, 11–15, 33–34

regula fidei, 43
representative leadership, 124
resurrection, 28

saint, 40
sanctification, 32–33
Scots Confession, 17, 20–21, 49, 139
Second Helvetic Confession, 63, 65, 69–70, 87, 142

teaching, 114
The Babylonian Captivity of the Church, 46

1. Church p7 - The renewal of the church is a gift for which we must wait & pray.

2. Creation p23 God continues to create & recreate the world, nature, men & women & societies as well.

3. Church p24 God's renovating, renewing, & restoring activity in the world.

4. Bible - The faithlessness of god's people & the faithfulness of god. p23

5. Providence p28 All human thought combined cannot fathom the mystery of god's love for people (and all creation)

6. Church p33 - The context of god's justifying & sanctifying activity.

7. Trinity p37 One godhead existing simultaneously in three modes of being.

8. Church p42 A light in the darkness.

9. Church p51 The "meetinghouse" where the community meets.

10. Church p76 The Church's five temptations.

11. Minister p99 Accountable to the father of the church & to the people of the church.

12. Church p107 A servant of the recovering, restoring grace of god

13. Prayer p122 An ongoing ministry of the whole community of faith.

✓

(1669)